BRITISH RAILWAYS

PAST and PRESENT

No 22

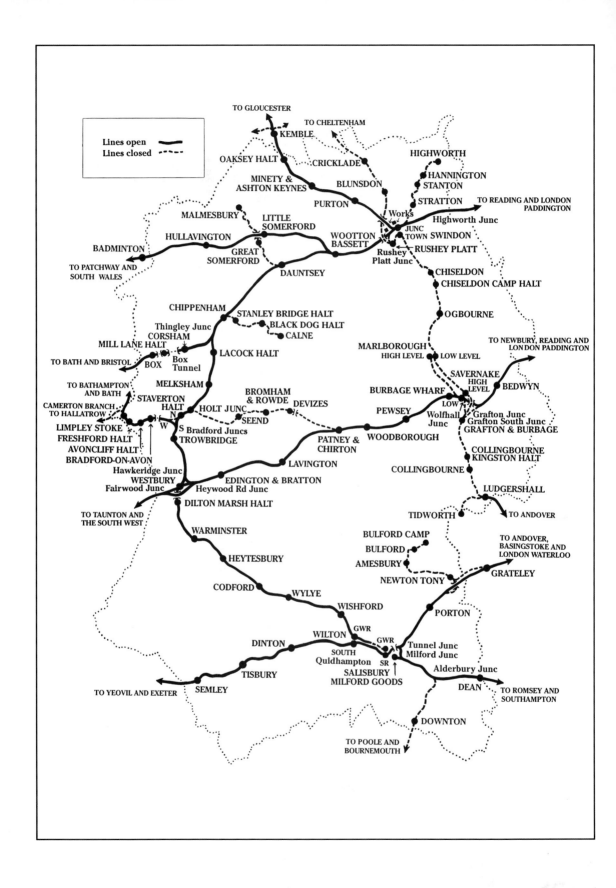

BRITISH RAILWAYS

PAST and PRESENT

No 22

Wiltshire

Graham Roose & Hugh Ballantyne

Past & Present Publishing Ltd

First published in October 1994

British Library Cataloguing in Publication Data

A catalogue record for this book is available from the British Library

ISBN 1 85895 049 X

Past & Present Publishing Ltd
Unit 5
Home Farm Close
Church Street
Wadenhoe
Peterborough PE8 5TE
Tel/fax (0832) 720440

Maps drawn by Christina Siviter

Printed and bound in Great Britain

SWINDON TOWN: A vintage postcard view of a railway scene typical of England's Edwardian period. Posted from Swindon to Dursley on 10 August 1914, the photograph shows the very neat layout of the principal M&SWJR station, looking south. The train at the platform is probably the 'North Express', which ran from Southampton to Cheltenham with through coaches to Birmingham, Leeds, Sheffield and Liverpool, and is hauled by one of the company's handsome 'Standard' Class 'L' passenger 4-4-0s. Between 1905 and 1914 the railway had nine of these engines, built by North British to the design of James Tyrrell, the M&SWJR Locomotive Superintendent. The station and railway south to Marlborough opened on 27 July 1881, and closed to passenger traffic on 11 September 1961, but its well-known old-fashioned privately managed refreshment room on the down platform remained open until the last licensee, Mrs Townsend, gave up in February 1965. Limited freight traffic continued until 1966, then final use in 1970/71 for stone trains off-loading materials for the construction of the nearby M4 motorway, the trains being trip-worked from Swindon Junction by locally based Class '08' shunters.

The retaining walls remain and the use to which the station site and track layout are being put as a light industrial estate is readily apparent. The path to the left on the course of the southbound line enables walkers to traverse 1.5 miles of the trackbed down to **Rushey Platt.** *Commercial postcard, Rev Brian Arman Collection/GR*

CONTENTS

BIBLIOGRAPHY

Bath to Weymouth Line *by Colin Maggs (Oakwood Press)*
Branch Lines of Wiltshire *by Colin Maggs (Alan Sutton)*
Brunel's Broad Gauge Railway *by Christopher Awdry (OPC)*
Calne Branch *by Colin Maggs (Wild Swan)*
GWR Country stations *by Chris Leigh (Ian Allan)*
Highworth Branch *by Smith & Heathcliffe (Wild Swan)*
Historical Survey of Great Western Engine Sheds *by E. Lyons (OPC)*
Historical Survey of Selected Great Western Stations *by R. H. Clark (OPC)*
History of the Great Western Railway *by MacDermot (GWR)*
Isambard Kingdom Brunel *by L. T. C. Rolt (Longmans)*
Joseph Locke - Railway Revolutionary *by N. W. Webster (Allen & Unwin)*
Locomotives of the GWR - *various volumes (RCTS)*
Locomotives of the Southern Railway Vol 2 *(RCTS)*
Midland and South Western Junction Railway *by Colin Maggs (David & Charles)*
Official Railway Junction Diagrams, 1915 edition *(Railway Clearing House)*

Pictorial Record of GWR Architecture *by Adrian Vaughan (OPC)*
Rail Centres - Swindon *by Colin Maggs (Ian Allan)*
Regional History of the Railways of Great Britain, Vol 1 *by D. St J. Thomas (Phoenix House Limited)*
Vol 2 *by H. P. White (Phoenix House Limited)*
Sectional Map of British Railways *(Ian Allan)*
The Western Before Beeching *by Chris Leigh (Ian Allan)*
The South Western Railway *by R. A. Williams (David & Charles)*
The GWR at Swindon Works *by Alan S. Peck (OPC)*
Thomas Brassey, Railway Builder *by Charles Walker (Frederick Muller)*
West of England Resignalling *by Adrian Vaughan (Ian Allan)*

Also:
Various issues of Bradshaw's Railway Timetable
The Railway Magazine *(IPC Magazines Limited)*
The Railway Observer *(the house magazine of the Railway Correspondence & Travel Society)*

SALISBURY (SR): The local enthusiasts were very pleased on this occasion to welcome a 'Britannia' to Salisbury, a Class never particularly common on this part of the system, especially as No 70004 *William Shakespeare* had once been one of the pair of immaculate 'Britannias' kept at Stewarts Lane to work the 'Golden Arrow' service to Dover. By the time this 'past' picture was taken steam was in decline on the Southern, but No 70004, now allocated to Stockport shed and de-named, came for a visit to South West England in August 1966 to work two enthusiasts' specials. Filling in time between those tours it was put to good use on a number of ordinary passenger services, including this arrival with a train from Waterloo.

A most fortuitous modern copy event 27 years later finds the prototype of the Class, No 70000 *Britannia*, in the same place, arriving with one of the 'Britannia Wessex' shuttle runs that took place between Eastleigh and Salisbury on 10 October 1993. The picture was taken with the help of Valerie Roose who held a magazine in the appropriate position to shield the camera from the sun that was shining directly into the lens as the exposure was made. *Keith Sanders/GR*

INTRODUCTION

Arguably this county represents the very best of rural England, despite being little known to outsiders. Yet it was in the forefront of the dawn of our ancient history and culture with Avebury Stones, Stonehenge and the man-made Silbury Hill, all dating back to at least 2,600 BC in the late Neolithic Age, the Roman occupation with its splendid Ermine Way traversing the county towards Cirencester, and later in Anglo-Saxon England becoming part of Wessex with its stories of the Arthurian Legends lost in the mists of time around Amesbury.

Geophysically the county has interesting contrasts and distinct regions within its boundaries. To the north, east and west of Swindon lie the gentle undulations of the agriculturally rich pastureland noted in its time, before EEC bureaucrats and butter mountains, as fine dairy and milk-producing country. South of Swindon are the Marlborough Downs and Savernake Forest; these downlands have revealed evidence of early settlements safe from the dense and dangerous forests of the lowland country. Southwards one passes the watershed of streams that feed into the Bristol Avon, while those to the south, as one enters the great chalk uplands of Salisbury Plain, flow to the Hampshire Avon. Again there is much evidence of our prehistoric past and, except where the Army, understandably, requires some areas for its military ranges and training grounds, the Plain has vast acreages of near treeless areas given over to the large-scale production of cereal crops.

Throughout history transportation has of course played its part. Prehistoric tracks across the upland Downs, followed by the Roman road and its branches, later the Bath Road, which provided a perilous stagecoach route from London to Bath and Bristol, pre-date the railway. Canals also left their mark, with the Thames & Severn in the north and the Kennet & Avon linking the river Avon at Bath with the Thames at Reading providing direct waterways right across England.

All this preempted the promoters of the Great Western Railway and their Engineer, Mr I. K. Brunel, who surveyed and built the line that swept east to west across the county following the Vale of the White Horse to the north of the Marlborough Downs before passing close to the tiny village of Swindon, then downhill from Wootton Bassett to Dauntsey and through the limestone escarpment and Box Tunnel to the county boundary just east of Bath. This was soon followed by a branch from Swindon to Kemble and Gloucester in 1841, the Wilts, Somerset & Weymouth Railway in the west, and a long arm of the Berks & Hants Extension Railway, which reached Devizes in 1862.

In the south or the county railways progressed westwards from Eastleigh to Salisbury, and this was quickly followed when that important ecclesiastical city was connected with the direct lines to London, Yeovil and eventually Exeter, by 1860. As the Railway Mania progressed branch lines proliferated, and the Midland & South Western Junction Railway completed its direct north-south route through the heart of the county. Early in the 20th century the War Office agreed to a railway on the south-east side of Salisbury Plain to Bulford, at about the same time that the Great Western was building its new direct route 'cut-off' lines.

Until the 1950s the pattern of railways was, with minor exceptions, completely stabilised, but when the effect of road competition made itself felt the railway management seemingly did little at the time to combat the serious threat and the effect it was to have. Today only the three main east-west routes of the original Great Western lines, one being the modern successor to the Berks & Hants, and the rival London & South Western Railway route in the south remain open, but with virtually no intermediate minor stations. Including the line from

Swindon to Kemble, the South Wales Direct route and the one line that retains a few small country stations, that from Bath to Trowbridge, Westbury and Salisbury, it means there are only 15 places in the county where passengers can join trains.

Other than truncated portions of the branch from Highworth Junction and Ludgershall towards Tidworth, all the former branch lines have been closed, and there is virtually no freight traffic generated other than limited business at Swindon, the largest town in the county, English China Clay at Quidhampton and some military traffic to Ludgershall and Dinton. However, the through routes that remain are at least flourishing, with modern trains providing frequent and regular-interval passenger services.

During the time that this book was in preparation, locomotive-hauled trains ceased on the Salisbury to Exeter line and have been replaced by Network SouthEast 'Turbo' Class '159' units providing a high standard of comfort, as do the Class '158' 'Express Sprinters' extensively used on the Bath-Salisbury-Southampton route. We can only hope that the future for these surviving railways is bright, and that with the advent of privatised railway management and the opening of the Channel Tunnel there will be new opportunities to expand and generate much more freight business and a progressive move towards reducing the huge volume of road-borne heavy goods traffic that our country now endures.

Author's note and Acknowledgements

When the publishers first broached the subject of Wiltshire in this series it was a happy coincidence that the two authors, as are many others in the series so far, not only regular photographers of the railway scene today but also participating members of the photographic portfolios of the Railway Correspondence and Travel Society. Our teaming up also had the benefit that Graham lives on the spot in Bradford-on-Avon and was thus well placed to plan the photography of the present-day scenes. Without exception all the present day pictures are Graham's work.

Hugh, now resident in North Staffordshire, originates from Bath, just over the county boundary, and in steam days was an active photographer in the area, and having extensive recall and knowledge of the county in the pre-Beeching era is responsible for the text which appears in this book.

However, neither of us could have hoped to complete this volume without the help and courtesy of many people, including photographers for the 'past' pictures and land-owners who kindly gave consent for us to enter their private property for Graham to obtain the 'present' pictures. We would particularly like to thank Maurice Arlett at Holt Junction, Rev Brian Arman, Mike Barnsley, David Bartholomew, Tim Bryan at Swindon Museum, Richard James, Rex Kennedy, Editor of *Steam Days*, Donald Lovelock at Calne, Colin Maggs, Simon Neave at Savernake High Level, Richard Pelham and Martin Smith.

We much appreciate the permission given by Gary Bond, Site Manager, Tarmac, Swindon, for access to Swindon Works site, and likewise the assistance given by Alan Wild who so carefully ascertained the present-day locations within that complex.

We also extend thanks to the individual photographers of the 'past' scenes, all of whom are acknowledged in the text against their particular pictures.

Thanks for the printing of the many negatives made or selected for use in this volume go to Geoff Dowling (another author in this series) and Derek Mercer.

Finally, but certainly not least, our thanks go to Madeleine Brown of Stoke-on-Trent, whose expertise on the word processor produced quality typing of our efforts.

Hugh Ballantyne, Eccleshall
Graham Roose, Bradford-on-Avon

Swindon

SWINDON JUNCTION (1): At the west end of the station platforms protecting the junction of the Bristol main line and the line to Gloucester stood Swindon West Box. It was opened in 1913 to replace two earlier signal boxes and was the largest in the area with 174 levers. Running into the station pass the box is No 2920 *Saint David* arriving from the Gloucester line with an SLS special from Birmingham on 15 June 1952. By that time the 77 Churchward 'Saints' were down to their last eight, but this engine was the last to go, being withdrawn from Hereford shed in October 1953. Despite the ugly headboard and BR lined black livery, the elegant lines of the locomotive are readily apparent; but this and the historical significance of this two-cylinder express design was not enough for it to be preserved, and the Class became extinct.

An enormous change has taken place at this important railway junction, with track severely rationalised, all the mechanical signalling gone, the buildings forming part of the carriage works on the south side demolished, and the land given over to car parking.

The clearest evidence for exact comparison in this 13 April 1994 view is the tall spire of St Mark's Church in the right background behind the passing HST. This church was built on donated land and consecrated in 1845 close by the GWR railway village (see page 13) for the benefit of the spiritual needs of the railway workers living in what was called the New Town. *R. C. Riley/GR*

SWINDON JUNCTION (2): This view shows the station looking east in the direction of London on 28 April 1963, with the permanent buildings designed by Brunel and brought into use in July 1842, 19 months after the railway had reached the town. The buildings consisted of two three-storey stone structures, one on each platform; the latter were designed as islands to enable easy interchange between Bristol and Gloucester line trains. To reduce capital expenditure the Great Western Directors contracted with Messrs J. & C. Rigby, the building contractors, to lease back the station in consideration of the Company stopping all passenger trains at Swindon for 10 minutes for refreshments, no other such stops between Paddington and Bristol being allowed. The building in the centre of the picture on the down island platform had once contained coffee and sitting rooms at platform level and a hotel on the upper floors, and had been at one time connected to the up platform on the left by a covered footbridge. The refreshment stop covenant in the lease caused much annoyance to the GWR, and it was not until 1895 that the Company was able to buy the lease for £100,000. This picture shows No 6018 *King Henry VI* on arrival with an SLS special from Birmingham Snow Hill to commemorate a last journey by a 'King' Class locomotive.

There is a completely different perspective on 20 June 1994, as the main part of the old down island platform has gone together with the Brunel station building upon it, and all passenger facilities have been concentrated on the up island platform since March 1968. Two through platforms are available and a short bay at the west end used by local trains to Gloucester or Westbury. Dominating the scene behind No 60063 *James Murray*, passing through on a Colnbrook to Waterstone empty oil tank train, is a multi-storey office block called Signal Point, but quite out of keeping with Mr Brunel's original style of architecture! *Hugh Ballantyne/GR*

SWINDON JUNCTION (3): This picture was taken close to the running lines outside A Shop on 29 September 1957, looking towards the station as No 5066 *Sir Felix Pole* passes its birthplace on the down main line with the 12.30 (Sundays) Paddington to Weston-super-Mare express. Behind the tender is the spire of St Mark's Church, the Locomotive Works are to the left of picture, and on the other side behind the train were railway timber stores and carriage works. No 5066 was built in July 1937 as *Wardour Castle*, was renamed in April 1956 in honour of the GWR's General Manager from 1921 to 1929, and in June 1959, after this picture was taken, was fitted with a double chimney, being finally withdrawn in September 1962.

The modern scene shows that most of the railway facilities have been removed, leaving just three tracks, MAS colour light signalling and relay boxes on the right covered in graffiti as an HST heads west working the 14.00 Paddington to Swansea service on 25 March 1994. The spire of St Mark's Church now shares part of the skyline with the multi-storey building seen in the previous photograph. *Hugh Ballantyne/GR*

SWINDON (NEW TOWN): In 1840 Daniel Gooch wrote to Brunel reporting on his favoured location for a repair depot on the new Great Western Railway. He advised Swindon, and in February 1841, with the prior approval of Brunel, the Directors decided 'to provide an engine establishment at Swindon. . . circumstances render it necessary for the building of cottages etc for the many persons employed in the service of the Company'. Designed by Sir Matthew Digby Wyatt (the architect of Paddington station), 300 'cottages' were provided by the GWR for the workers at the new factory on the south side of the line. In 1845 four streets, partly shown on the left side of this photograph, were completed leading off Emlyn Square, followed by four more to the east of the square shortly afterwards. This was an usually benevolent act by the company in those times, and the houses even had small front gardens and at the back a wash-house and privy. They were built by the local firm J. & C. Rigby & Co at their own expense, the builder recovering the cost from rents collected by the GWR. In the right background is the Mechanics Institute, built in Tudor style at about the same time, to provide education facilities and a library. At the end of the square is the southern boundary wall of the Works, and in this fine vintage scene the homeward-bound workers have emerged from the main entrance opposite the end of the Mechanics Institute. The photograph is undated, but from the style of dress is likely to have been taken between 1900 and 1920 on a sunny mid-day in springtime when the men were leaving for their dinner break.

Today the houses are owned by Thamesdown Borough Council and are tastefully restored externally and internally with bathrooms and new kitchens. The two corner pubs remain in business, the nearest being the Cricketers Arms on the corner of Exeter Street, clearly visible in both pictures; behind, on the corner of Bathampton Street, is the Bakers Arms. On the right and now protected from vandals by a strong metal fence stands the Mechanics Institute, which on 21 January 1994, when this photograph was taken, was not in use.
Rev Brian Arman Collection/BR

SWINDON WORKS: Arguably the most impressive locomotive workshops in the world, Swindon in its heyday had a reputation for building and repairing locomotives and carriages second to none. Much of the locomotive work took place in the huge A Shop (see also the photographs on the front cover), visible on the right of this 1 December 1963 picture outside which the two identifiable locomotives are Nos 4555 and 6000. At that time No 4555, which had been built at the Works in January 1924, had just been withdrawn; it was subsequently sold to the late Mr P. B. Whitehouse and went into preservation service on the Dart Valley Railway. It currently works on the nearby associated Paignton & Dartmouth Steam Railway. The famous No 6000 *King George V*, built at Swindon in June 1927, seen with its bell removed for safe custody, had been withdrawn in December 1962. It remained at Swindon Works until 1964, when finally a decision was made to preserve it; ownership was transferred to Swindon Corporation, and it was put into store. In 1968 it was loaned to cider-makers H. P. Bulmer Limited and, following overhaul by Messrs A. R. Adams & Sons, Newport, it was displayed at Hereford. Very appropriately, on 2 October 1971 it led the 'return to steam' on BR metals following the three-year steam ban with a triumphant run from Hereford to Tyseley via Severn Tunnel Junction, Swindon and Oxford. After 20 years of service on main-line preservation runs it is now on non-active display in Swindon Railway Museum.

Perhaps one of the saddest sights of any in this series of 'Past and Present' books is the now bare and cleared demolition site upon which the once magnificent A Shop once stood. The building was demolished during 1988, leaving the concrete access road, a few rails and the weighing and balancing shop in the left background as stark reminders of glories past. The official title of the latter was Weighbridge House, and being the only surviving 20th-century-constructed building of the Works complex, it is hoped that this small but once important structure will be allowed to remain as a reminder of the later architectural period. *R. A. Lissenden/GR*

SWINDON SHED (1) was situated on the east side of the line to Gloucester, and the building on the left in this picture formed the original part opened in 1871 as a standard gauge shed; the broad gauge shed was on a different site. In 1908 the building on the right was added, which was a roundhouse with 27 roads radiating off the central turntable. This 9 May 1964 picture shows Nos 7022 *Hereford Castle*, 7927 *Willington Hall* and 46251 *City of Nottingham*. The 'Coronation' Class 'Pacific' was a distinguished visitor, resting on shed during a lull in its duties of hauling the RCTS 'East Midlander No 7' special, which it had brought from Nottingham to Didcot. While the special went on to Eastleigh, No 46251 ran to Swindon to await the returning train to take it back to its starting point later in the day. The shed was closed on 2 November 1964 and demolished in 1971.

Thanks are due to the knowledge of long-standing Swindon railwayman Mr Alan Wild we were able to find the present-day position for the past scene on 13 April 1994. All trace of the railway has disappeared and the local shed site now forms part of the Hawksworth Industrial Estate. *Hugh Ballantyne/GR*

SWINDON SHED (2): A fine picture of the coaling stage on 20 September 1964 with its 80,000-gallon capacity water tank over it. Access for coal wagons was by means of shunting up the ramp visible to the right. The coal stage was of standard Great Western construction and had the usual corrugated cladding lean-to for protection of the coal wagons. Of the three locomotives visible parked on the non-delivery side of the stage, the Class '56XX' 0-6-2T looks to be out service, the 'Hall' Class is unidentified, while No 7816 *Frilsham Manor* retains 'GWR' initials on its 3,500-gallon tender 17 years after nationalisation of the company. No 7816 was built at Swindon in January 1939 and withdrawn in November 1965.

Again thanks to Mr Wild's detailed knowledge of Swindon's railway layout, on 25 March 1994 this warehouse unit was located, which stands on the site of the coal stage and part of the loco yard. *R. A. Lissenden/GR*

GWR main line

WOOTTON BASSETT: This view, looking from the west end of the down platform towards the junction where the Bristol and Badminton lines bifurcate, sees a rather dirty No 5094 *Tretower Castle* working the 08.30 (SO) Bristol to Paddington on a dull 25 March 1961. At the platform end is a fine three-post bracket signal with, left to right, arms routing down home to down goods loop, down main inner home above down main intermediate distant, and down South Wales intermediate distant. The home signals were controlled by the East signal box, just visible behind the bracket, and the distants were cautions for signals controlled by the West box. The station opened on 30 July 1841, but was substantially rebuilt for the opening of the South Wales direct line on 1 January 1903. It was closed to passengers on 4 January 1965 and general goods traffic ten months later.

Today access at platform level is not possible, and this 17 November 1993 picture was taken from the road overbridge that was at the east end of the platforms. The extensive railway land remains evident, but the station has been completely demolished. One up relief line remains, just visible behind the approaching London-bound HST. *Hugh Ballantyne/GR*

CHIPPENHAM (1): A truly 'Great Western' scene on Mr Brunel's original line of railway, which was opened here on the broad gauge on 31 May 1841. With clear signals through the station, No 1006 *County of Cornwall* approaches the down platform from the north-east on the sunny evening of 3 May 1953 displaying Class 3 lamps for vans or 'perishable' traffic. The train appears to be mainly empty milk tanks, no doubt *en route* from London to West of England milk depots. Behind the engine is the substantial goods shed; to the rear of the train the Calne branch turned eastwards off the main line. No 1006 was built at Swindon in November 1945, not named until April 1948, later fitted with a double chimney, and withdrawn from service in September 1963.

As one would expect on today's railway using modern track maintenance machinery, the down main line is beautifully aligned but all other evidence of the extensive railway facilities and track layout seen in the 'past' view have gone in this 15 December 1993 view. The land on which the goods shed and down sidings stood has either been sold off or, nearer the station, forms part of the station car park. *D. Lovelock/GR*

CHIPPENHAM (2): Looking into the station from the west end on 15 June 1955 we see the buildings and layout, which had been modified at the turn of the century when the old train shed was removed. The 'King', No 6024 *King Edward I*, is standing at the down main platform working the 5.00 pm Swindon to Bristol local train, a regular Swindon Works running-in turn for main-line locomotives ex-workshops or brand new. Hence the reason for this most prestigious express locomotive, in immaculate condition, on such a menial train; it was being tested after major overhaul in the Works. The platform on the left is the south side of the island and was operated as two bays, this end being Platform 2 for Westbury and Weymouth trains. The far end was called Platform 4 and was used by Calne branch trains, while the north side of the island (not visible), then, as now, is the up main platform. The footbridge nearest the camera was a public footbridge that crossed over the station and was not used by passengers. Chippenham was an extremely busy station, especially so during the Second World War with added service personnel and munitions traffic and workers in the area; a reminder of those times are the bicycle sheds on the right-hand side. It is pleasing to note that although No 6024 was withdrawn from service in June 1962, it was purchased from Barry scrapyard and is now restored and passed for running on BR-approved routes.

In February 1976 major track alterations were carried out, and these are visible in the 2 June 1994 picture. The two former bays used by Calne and Westbury line trains had been out of use for some years, and in preparation for HST services the down main line was realigned to the south side of the island platform and the old down main passing Platform 1 was lifted; this has resulted in all passengers having to cross the station footbridge from the main entrance. Part of the station offices on the old Platform 1 are visible in the centre of this view, and today the single-storey slated-roof building in Bath stone is Grade 2 listed. The other noticeable alteration is the removal of the bicycle shed from the old down platform. The HST is standing at the down platform working as the 12.15 Paddington to Bristol service. *Mark B. Warburton/GR*

CHIPPENHAM (3): This picture, taken from the north side of Chippenham station and looking south-west towards Thingley Junction, is full of railway interest. The down 'Merchant Venturer', 11.15 Paddington to Bristol, passes through the station non-stop *en route* to Bath and Bristol hauled by No 7024 *Powis Castle* on 8 June 1953

As we have seen, the old down main line has now gone and only the island platform at Chippenham is served by trains. A down HST, the 08.15 Paddington to Bristol service, draws out of the platform, next stop Bath, on 13 April 1994. Various buildings in the background are still recognisable, but all the sidings and crossovers in the 'past' picture have been removed. *G. F. Heiron/GR*

CHIPPENHAM SHED: Considering that this was only a sub-shed to Swindon it was a remarkably impressive build-ing, containing three roads and measuring 95 by 50 feet. It was located opposite the divergence of the Calne branch from the main line, east of the station and on the north side of the line; it is believed to have opened in about 1858 and remained in use until March 1964. It usually housed half a dozen or more Pannier tanks and auto-train-fitted '14XXs'. A Pannier tank, in steam, peers out of the middle track of the shed in this view.

Only scrub and bushes on the wasteland are evident on 13 June 1994, and it is not possible to visualise the quite large engine shed that once stood here. The photograph was taken from the trackbed of the old Calne branch looking straight across the main running lines. *T. W. Nicholls/GR*

THINGLEY SIDINGS: Two miles south-west of Chippenham extensive sidings were constructed for military and government traffic, the first of which were laid *circa* 1937. During the Second World War they were extended as vast traffic was generated by one of the largest and most secret underground ammunition works and stores that was located nearby. Government traffic continued long after the war, although on a steadily declining basis, but as can be seen here, on 4 August 1959, the railway facilities were still extensive.

Today a few sidings remain in situ but are not in regular use, and a covered area has been provided at a raised platform on the left, superseding the former ground-level facilities. On the right an HST is approaching on the down line heading towards Bath, and in the right background can be seen the line to Bradford Junction. 1 June 1994. *Colin G. Maggs/GR*

CORSHAM: Main-line steam disappeared from the Bristol route in 1963, having been superseded by the Western Region diesel-hydraulics that continued to dominate the Paddington-Bristol services for another ten years or so. Seen in the heyday of the 'Westerns' in September 1969, D1059 *Western Empire*, in blue livery, reaches the top of the 1 in 100 climb from Box Tunnel as it passes the disused goods shed at Corsham station hauling an up express to Paddington. The station had been closed in January 1965.

The goods shed building still remains in commercial use and on 13 June 1994 the only apparent changes in 25 years are the removal of the trailing crossover, further development on the hillside above the railway and the seemingly inevitable increase in vegetation on the cutting sides. There are no scheduled locomotive-hauled passenger trains on this route today, all main services such as this 14.15 Bristol to Paddington being operated by HSTs. *Paul Strong/GR*

BOX TUNNEL: By May 1841 there was one final link to be forged to complete Brunel's great imperial iron road from London westwards to Bath and Bristol, and it was the most difficult link of all. Nearly two miles long, Box Tunnel at that time was by far the largest railway tunnel attempted, and a quite amazing engineering feat when one considers that it was accomplished by men and horses working by candlelight and the power of gunpowder. Commenced in September 1836, it was 3,212 yards long on a falling gradient of 1 in 100 towards Bath; it was completed in June 1841, some nine months later than originally stipulated. It cost, for those times, a staggering £6.5 million, but was a tribute to Brunel's ability and determination and stands as a fine memorial. Its western portal emphasises the style and genius of Brunel in its decorative facade. It has rusticated quoins, acanthus leaf carved keystone, trusses beneath the cornice and ornamental balustrading on the parapet. Totally in keeping with the surroundings, one of the Great Western's premier express locomotives, No 6024 *King Edward I*, is emerging with the 5.00 pm local train from Swindon to Bristol on 15 June 1955. The same train, a Swindon Works running-in turn, has already been seen at Chippenham (page 19).

In recent times efforts have been made by a local civic society to restore and maintain this marvellous western

portal to its former glory, and the evening sunshine on the Bath stonework makes for a most pleasing sight. Unfortunately the vegetation, cut back on restoration, is being allowed to encroach again on the cutting slopes, so go soon if you wish for an unobstructed view of an HST emerging from beneath Box Hill; this is the 17.10 Paddington to Weston-super-Mare service on 25 June 1994. *Mark B. Warburton/GR*

BOX MIDDLE HILL TUNNEL: Half a mile to the west of Box Tunnel is the shorter Middle Hill Tunnel, just 200 yards long. This picture was taken from ground that had once formed part of the down goods yard of Box station, and shows D1737 approaching the western portal with the 11.40 Weston-super-Mare to Paddington train on 30 August 1965. Brunel designed many beautiful decorative facades for his tunnels, but this, together with Box opposite, are probably his finest. Like Box, this western portal shows another unique design with the arch divided into segments and a scroll pattern keystone. Pilasters rise to the parapet on each side of the arch and inset to each are the Roman style of fasces for final decoration.

On 15 December 1993 an HST forming the 12.15 Bristol-Paddington service approaches the western portal. The all too common excess lineside vegetation is evident, and it is a sad example of lack of care by BR civil engineering staff that they do not keep this further splendid architectural example of our railway heritage free of growth and saplings. *M. Mensing/GR*

MILL LANE HALT, BOX was located between the two tunnels, in a much more central position to the village than Box station itself. The halt was not opened until 31 March 1930, so the locals had to wait a mere 89 years for the railway to provide this convenient facility. On a cold winter's morning, 18 March 1961, immaculate 'Castle' No 5023 *Brecon Castle* draws away with the 06.40 Bristol to Swindon local train on the 1 in 120 gradient, shortly to steepen to 1 in 100 in Box Tunnel.

The halt has now disappeared and the view is blocked by the ugly pole and untidy field/garden boundary so that the approaching up HST has had to be photographed a little earlier than the corresponding 'past' picture. While the contents of the transport yard on the right seem to have changed, the low retaining wall and concrete post-and-wire fence remain. *Hugh Ballantyne/GR*

27

BOX STATION (1) was the intermediate wayside station on the section of the broad gauge line opened between Chippenham and Bath on 30 June 1841, and this photograph shows to good advantage the lovely Brunelian station building on the down platform and the standard lattice girder (with monogram) foot-bridge complete with awning that was provided here. It appears that the designs that Mr Brunel produced for Box in the earliest days of the Great Western Railway were the starting point for a standardised style of 'roadside' or 'wayside' station. Such types were designed to provide the usual railway station offices but no accommodation for the staff. Research indicates there may have been four styles, but Box, one of the first, had an awning supported on beams lying across the building and projecting from the walls to support the canopy that surrounded the building. Added to this was the low-pitched roof and decorative chimneys, and, being built in the local Bath stone, it blended perfectly into its surroundings. Running into the down platform is a DMU working as the 10.15 (SX) Swindon to Bristol all-stations train on the penultimate day of service, 1 January 1965.

It is not possible to align a direct comparison photograph today as the platforms and station have gone and thick vegetation is close to the track on both sides, making access impossible. This 5 May 1994 picture was taken from the A4 road overbridge immediately to the west of where the platforms had been and shows Class '37' Nos 37162 and 37038 heading down to Bath with the 6C13 11.21 Calvert to Bath and Westerleigh empty waste disposal train. *Hugh Ballantyne/GR*

BOX STATION (2): This second view was taken from a rarely photographed angle and shows the up side with No 1433 and two auto-trailers waiting to leave as the 8.25 am to Chippenham. This unusual working had commenced as the 7.25 am Calne to Chippenham, after which it ran as empty coaching stock to Box, ran round and formed this short main-line local working back, enabling people to get to work in Chippenham before 9.00 am.

On 26 April 1994 nothing remains visible on either side of the station site except undergrowth and trees. The attractive station building was demolished following closure on 2 January 1965. *D. Lovelock/GR*

Kemble line and the Highworth branch

PURTON is seen here on 29 May 1965, having closed to passengers six months previously on 2 November 1964 and to goods on 1 July 1963. This view, looking west from the minor road overbridge at the platform end (which also served as the station footbridge), shows the platforms cut back but the signal box still in use as a block post and the double track still in situ. Purton was the first station from Swindon on the Stroud and Gloucester main line and was opened as broad gauge in May 1841, being converted to standard gauge in 1872. The station underwent several alterations and the final somewhat plain flat-roofed main building on the down platform is visible. The train passing, hauled by No 4472 *Flying Scotsman*, was an RCTS special, the 'East Midlander No 8', which had

originated from Nottingham Midland and had travelled via Clapham Junction to Swindon for a Works and shed visit, finally returning to Nottingham, as seen here, via Gloucester and Derby.

Twenty-eight years later, in December 1993, the somewhat unattractive station building and part of the down platform survive, although looking the worse for wear, as part of the Station Garage, and surrounded by miscellaneous junk. The line from Swindon to Kemble has been singled. *M. Mensing/GR*

MINETY & ASHTON KEYNES: Despite the period appearance of this splendid view, with its two prewar-looking motor cars, the picture is dated 15 March 1952. It shows to good advantage the lovely Brunel style of 'roadside' station that survived, more or less intact, right from opening in 1841 to closure on 2 November 1964. Distinctive features of this handsome wayside building are the steeply pitched roof topped by the tall chimney with a canopy around the building supported on ornate brackets. Subsequent to its opening, the up platform was considerably extended under the road bridge.

Nowadays that lovely Brunel wayside station would surely have had a preservation order placed upon it, but no such thing happened following closure in 1964, so on 28 February 1994 we have this depressing scene with all aspects of the station and sidings almost totally destroyed. Just a remnant of the down platform remains visible, and the pub that stood in the station yard has been de-licensed and the brewery whose beers it sold in 1952 has long ceased to exist. The only consolation is that at least the single line is still well used by trains between Swindon and Gloucester and the road overbridge remains intact. *H. C. Casserley/GR*

OAKSEY HALT: Two miles north-west of Minety & Ashton Keynes on the 1 in 330 rise towards Kemble, a small halt was constructed at Oaksey. It had stone-built platforms on each line, but only a basic galvanised corrugated iron sheeting waiting shelter was provided on each platform. The halt was opened on 18 February 1929 and closed with the other intermediate stations between Kemble and Swindon on 2 November 1964. It was the most northerly point in Wiltshire at which passengers could join or alight from a train.

The view from the same road overbridge on 28 February 1994 shows how nature's vegetation and scrub has gained control, and by necessity the picture had to be taken in winter. Both platforms remain clearly visible, but the remaining single track has been realigned clear of the platform edges. *R. M. Casserley Collection/GR*

STRATTON was the first station along the Highworth branch, and just 1¹/₄ miles from the main line at Highworth Junction. When the branch opened in 1883 the village of Stratton St Margaret was quite separate from Swindon and presented a compact rural community. Situated in rich dairy-farming country, the branch, and this station in particular, generated substantial milk traffic, all of which was sent to depots in London. The churns were loaded into 'Siphon' vans, which, until the 1930s, went to Swindon behind an evening branch train and were shunted to be worked forward in a up milk train to London. This picture shows the station and yard from the excellent vantage point of the road overbridge. Great Western galvanised corrugated iron features strongly here: note the Type 'A' Shelter, a 'Pagoda', at the near end of the station building, which served as both parcels office and waiting room. Behind the main building is a small corrugated lock-up hut used for parcel storage, at the platform end is another galvanised corrugated iron hut for lamps, and, not least, a large similarly constructed goods shed on a platform facing the loop. By the time this picture was taken, development from Swindon was steadily moving towards Stratton.

The scene is totally unrecognisable on 28 February 1994, save for a few trees on the left. The road overbridge has been demolished and the old goods yard at this point forms the entrance to the Europa Industrial Estate. Behind this, residential development has moved up towards the former railway boundary. *D. Lovelock/GR*

CRICKLADE ROAD CROSSING: About half a mile north of Stanton, the next station on the branch, and on a falling gradient, the line crossed the Blunsdon to Highworth Road at Cricklade Road Crossing. Until 1928 a crossing-keeper was employed here, but thereafter it became an unmanned crossing operated by the fireman and guard of each train. On a bleak winter's day, 6 December 1952, with the landscape snow-covered, No 1467 stops at the gates with the 1.20 pm from Highworth to Swindon. Reflected in the window of the second, and last, coach of this little train is milepost $3^3/_4$ measured from Highworth Junction.

Forty two years later, on 9 February 1994, one of the level crossing gates remains in situ and the location is readily identifiable thanks to the tree on the left and the hedgerow of what has now become the B4019 road to Blunsdon. Not surprisingly the eastern railway boundary fence and milepost have disappeared and the trackbed of the branch is now contained within the adjacent field. *Hugh Ballantyne/GR*

HANNINGTON was the penultimate station on the branch, $4^1/_2$ miles from Swindon Junction and over a mile from the village it purported to serve. It was in a delightful location and the trees to the right of the single platform were noted for their profusion of bluebells in springtime. There had been a loop and one siding to the left of the Pannier tank, but these were removed in June 1959. On the extreme left can be seen the derelict remains of the sleeper-built platelayers' hut. This Gloucestershire Railway Society special of 31 March 1962 was returning from Highworth to Swindon hauled by No 1658. The branch was nominally closed to passengers in February 1953, but BR staff trains continued until 3 August 1962 when the branch closed to all traffic north of Kingsdown Road Junction.

Back to nature with a vengeance! The site of the pretty little station is now a farm manure dump, and

although the railway boundary line remains clearly discernible to the left, the line of ragged trees on the skyline has also gone. 19 January 1994. *J. Spencer Gilks/GR*

Badminton line and the Malmesbury branch

LITTLE SOMERFORD: As is well recorded, in the 1890s the Great Western planned new railways to give shorter routes and faster train services. One of the most important new lines was the Bristol & South Wales Direct between Wootton Bassett and Patchway, a distance of 29¾ miles, often known as the Badminton line. This made the route from Paddington to Severn Tunnel Junction 10 miles shorter, and with less severe gradients, than the old route via Bath. The first section of the new line as far as Badminton was opened on 1 January 1903, and two new standard styles were used for the intermediate stations, some having up and down relief lines through the platforms with the up and down fast lines in between, as seen here at Little Somerford. Coming under the covered footbridge is No 5066 *Wardour Castle* on an up train heading towards Swindon *circa* 1954. The station was closed to passengers on 3 April 1961.

The only traces on 13 June 1994 are the platform edges, the once attractive station and track layout having been swept away. The 85¾ milepost has been repositioned in the formation of the up relief line as an HST passes working the 13.32 Swansea to Paddington service. *D. Lovelock/GR*

HULLAVINGTON was the third station westwards on the Badminton line, 11 miles from Wootton Bassett, and the last of the three intermediate stations along the line in Wiltshire. This view is looking westwards on 9 July 1959, where the railway is making a long steady 1 in 300 climb from near Little Somerford to Badminton, high up on the southern end of the Cotswold Hills.

The station, closed on 3 April 1961, has completely disappeared by 20 June 1994, but the yard is occupied as commercial premises. However, the down loop line, behind the platform in the past picture, is still in use today. *H. C. Casserley/GR*

GREAT SOMERFORD was the first station on the Malmesbury branch, and north-west of the station the line crossed a minor road at Kingsmead crossing, seen here behind the Gloucester Railway Society special hauled by 0-6-0PT No 1658 heading back to the main line junction from Malmesbury on 31 March 1962. Originally this market town was determined, as so many others throughout England, to be connected to the railway system, and consequently the Malmesbury Railway was opened in December 1877 connecting with the GWR at Dauntsey. Following the construction of the direct Bristol & South Wales Railway by the GWR in 1903 a temporary connection was laid from the branch at this point eastwards to the new line at Little Somerford. This reduced the length of the branch from $6^{1}/_{2}$ to $3^{3}/_{4}$ miles, and eventually a permanent line was laid and came into regular service in

July 1933, so the section from Kingsmead Crossing to Dauntsey was closed. Gradually bus competition saw off the passenger service, which ceased on 8 September 1951, but substantial goods traffic remained, so much so that the daily freight eventually became diesel-hauled by Class '03' shunters from Swindon. However, the usual story of lack of business incentive prevailed, and even what had appeared to be lucrative goods traffic ceased to be conveyed by rail on 11 November 1962.

Today the crossing-keeper's house is still a residence and the track formation can be identified, but the land has reverted to its historic use - agriculture - and a line of trees is the demarcation of the former eastern railway boundary. 19 January 1994. *J. Spencer Gilks/GR*

MALMESBURY SHED: A delightful study of little Collett '58XX' Class non-auto-fitted 0-4-2T No 5802 resting outside Malmesbury shed on 18 August 1957 during a break in its duties as branch goods engine and shunter for the daily pick-up goods train from Swindon. Although the loco shed had ceased to house a branch engine in 1951 when the line lost its passenger service, facilities remained at the shed including use of the water tank behind the engine. Despite the Great Western having been nationalised for nearly ten years, No 5802 still retains the time-honoured 'GWR' lettering on its side tanks. It was built at Swindon in January 1933 and withdrawn in December 1958.

Unusually for a present-day scene there is less vegetation visible as the trees behind where the water tank once stood have gone and the land behind utilised as part of a tyre-fitting centre. The south end doors of the loco shed have been blocked off but the shed building remains very much in use on 19 January 1994. *Hugh Davies/GR*

Calne branch

STANLEY BRIDGE HALT was the first stop from Chippenham on this little branch line to Calne, although the halt was not opened until 3 April 1905. It was situated in lush pastoral land surrounded by scattered farms, and little else, so not surprisingly collection of milk churns here was substantial in the pre-motor-lorry era. The halt, with its 'Pagoda'-type waiting shelter, provided minimal but sufficient facilities, not least three ornate oil-lamps and a large nameboard, all seen here in this picture taken from the adjoining minor road overbridge and looking south-east towards Calne.

The lovely rural landscape has changed little and, as the line was at ground level in this vicinity, it is not surprising that little evidence of a railway remains. Certainly anyone looking over the bridge here and not knowing of the former existence of the railway would be hard pressed to visualise that trains had once passed here. Only the northern boundary of the line remains defined, and the once delightful halt has just become part of a grass-covered paddock and field. *Douglas Thompson, P. Q. Treloar Collection/GR*

BLACK DOG HALT (1): Perhaps the most unusual halt or stopping place in the county's railways system was Black Dog Halt, one of two intermediate stops on the 4$\frac{1}{2}$-mile branch from Chippenham to Calne. This halt was built as a private station to serve Bowood House, the nearby residence of the Marquis of Lansdowne. Opened in 1875, it did not appear in public timetables, although the public were allowed to use it. The Marquis provided the Station Master with a house, seen in the left background, and gave him 4 tons of coal annually to heat it! No station nameboard was provided until it was transferred to BR in September 1952, but the simple timber building seen on the platform remained in use, and this view is looking towards Calne.

The former Station Master's house and other estate house, together with the loading platform in the siding, are still visible on 16 February 1994. The platform remains hidden in the bushes on the right, and the trackbed is used as a path and access way. *D. Lovelock/GR*

42

BLACK DOG HALT (2): Looking now towards Chippenham on 9 September 1965, a three-car DMU leaves the halt working as the 13.00 from Calne to Chippenham. The picture shows the sylvan setting of this little station, but the siding seen in the picture opposite has been removed. Vehicular access to the station and houses from the A4 Bath Road was by means of the approach road seen on the right.

The access road to the houses remains very much in use, as can be seen on the right of the 16 February 1994 view, and the trackbed is clearly discernible as it is used as a footpath. The platform lies hidden under the trees on the extreme left of this photograph. *Paul Strong/GR*

BLACK DOG HALT (3): A real 'period picture' of the railway overbridge on the north-west side of the station by which the Calne branch crossed the main London to Bath Great West Road. The prominent railway notice on the Calne side of the bridge advises that this access is the carriage approach to the station and that foot passengers should go under the railway bridge.

The railway bridge was demolished in 1971, and now having all the symptoms of a modern road, the A4 has been slightly realigned, kerbed and marked with a single continuous centre line restricting overtaking by east-bound traffic *en route* to Calne. The prominent railway notice has been down-graded to one of the modem 'visual'-type footpath signs so popular today, pointing towards the footpath on the trackbed of the former branch on 16 February 1994. *P. Q. Treloar Collection/GR*

CALNE (1): The approaches to the station looking east towards the buffer-stops. The signal box and platform are on the extreme left, and this picture gives a good view of the extensive goods yard with its eight sidings, goods shed, cattle pens and 5 ton 18 cwt yard crane on the right. The photograph was taken *circa* 1962 at a busy time when the local goods engine was shunting the yard, hence the stance of the shunter with his pole on the right watching the movement of the Pannier tank (not visible) during the operations.

Despite the considerable volume of goods and perishable traffic generated from this station over the years, the Western Region allowed it all to trickle away and goods traffic ceased on 2 November 1963. By 21 March 1994 everything has gone, replaced by the office building constructed across part of the station site, with much of the rest given over to car parking. *D. Lovelock/GR*

CALNE (2): This small Wiltshire town had been a staging post on the Bath Road in coaching days before the railway era, but was bypassed when the Great Western Railway was completed between London, Bath and Bristol. The town was a busy place with numerous mills and C. & T. Harris (Calne) Limited's factory, famous for its pies and bacon and whose business was the largest of its kind in England. Eventually a broad gauge branch 5¼ miles long was built from Chippenham and opened for goods on 29 October 1863, and to passengers five days later. Despite its short length it was a busy line with Harris's providing much regular business. The negative attitude of BR prevailing in the 1950s and '60s affected this line, traffic declined in the 1960s and the branch closed to all traffic on 20 September 1965. This picture was taken from the buffer-stops and shows the quite substantial station buildings and the long single platform just before closure. The Government paid the GWR to extend the platform in 1942 to accommodate the eight coach trains required for transporting large numbers

46

of RAF personnel to the training camps a few miles away at Compton Bassett and Yatesbury. At the same time the timber building by the nameboard was added and became the booking office and waiting room, which had previously been in the main building on the right. On 4 September 1965, in the final weeks of the branch, a three-car DMU is leaving as the 4.12 pm to Chippenham, and the run-down state as compared with the previous view is evident, with all the sidings lifted and the water tank on top of the store building, beyond the booking office, removed.

Thanks to the help of local resident Mr D. Lovelock, the photographer was advised that here on 21 March 1994 he was standing at the location of the buffer-stops - otherwise it is virtually impossible now to identify the position of the railway features. This end of the station and run-round loop has become part of an agricultural merchant's warehouse. *Hugh Ballantyne/GR*

Thingley Junction to
Limpley Stoke and Trowbridge

LACOCK HALT: At the turn of the century the Great Western was seeking ways to economise on the operation of local train services and, in urban areas, also to combat the rise of the new tramway systems. The company partly solved the problem with the introduction of steam railmotors, a small steam engine incorporated into one end of a passenger coach. However, in about 1905, to overcome some of their obvious shortcomings, the company started to use small tank locomotives coupled to a trailer coach which contained facilities for the driver to operate and drive the train when it was being propelled by the locomotive. The scheme was quickly developed, and to cater for the potential traffic numerous simple unstaffed halts with minimal facilities were built. On the line between Thingley Junction and Bradford four such halts were opened in 1905. The first of these, seen here on 4 August

1959, was Lacock Halt, opened on 16 October 1905. This view, looking north, shows the outer signals protecting Thingley Junction, the short platforms with the classic GWR corrugated sheeted 'Pagoda' waiting shelters on each side and prominent nameboards.

The large ploughed field looks as well tended on 26 April 1994 as it had been 35 years before. The up platform remains but all trace of the 'Pagodas', nameboards, fencing and down platform have gone as DMU No 153380 comes south on the now single line, working as the 17.56 Swindon to Westbury service. *Colin G. Maggs/GR*

MELKSHAM, looking south, photographed on the last day of service, 16 April 1966. This was the only intermediate station on that part of the Wilts, Somerset & Weymouth Railway between Thingley Junction and Trowbridge when the line was opened as a broad gauge railway on 5 September 1848. The station was built in Brunel's 'roadside' style and its design is attributed to plans of Geddes/Nolloth, two of Brunel's important and well-trained assistants. The railway became a useful connecting line between the main Paddington-Bristol route and that from Reading to Weymouth and Taunton. Even so, local passenger trains were withdrawn from 18 April 1966 and this picture shows the last 5.02 pm from Westbury to Chippenham, a three-car DMU in green livery, standing in the up platform. A year later, in February 1967, the line was singled between Thingley Junction and Bradford Junction.

Although the line, albeit singled, remained in use for through trains, it was not until 1981, following the introduction of a summer train service from Swindon to Weymouth, that interest in reviving a local service was proposed. It is pleasing to report that on 13 May 1985 this simplified station was reopened using the old down platform. Only a very limited service is provided, literally one train each way on Mondays to Fridays, but at least it is better than it was! Here on 13 April 1994 the northbound service is arriving at the station to collect passengers travelling on single-car unit No 153362 working as the 07.40 Frome to Swindon service. *Hugh Ballantyne/GR*

STAVERTON HALT: Just over a mile south-west of Holt Junction and close to Bradford Junction, this halt was opened on 16 October 1905 and was conveniently placed for the village of the same name and a nearby Nestle's Creamery. This picture, looking north-east towards Chippenham on 25 September 1960, shows the simple wooden construction of the two platforms and waiting shelters. The halt closed with all the other intermediate stations on 18 April 1966.

Other than part of the down platform hidden in the bushes on the right and traces of the path on the left, little evidence of the halt remains on 11 April 1994 as unit No 153374 traverses the single track in the shallow cutting overrun with brambles, making its way north as the 07.40 Frome to Swindon train. *H. C. Casserley/GR*

BRADFORD NORTH JUNCTION: At Bradford Junction the lines from Bathampton and Thingley Junction converged to run south towards Westbury. On 10 March 1895 an east-west curve was opened giving direct access between these two lines, thereby enabling trains between Chippenham, Bath and Bristol to have a diversionary route avoiding the use of Box Tunnel during maintenance periods. In addition to the track, signal boxes were provided at the west and north junctions, which required the existing Bradford Junction box to be renamed Bradford South Junction. The new curve was singled in February 1967, and this 15 April 1973 picture shows Class '47' No 1940 approaching North Junction from West Junction with the 08.20 Weston-super-Mare to Paddington train diverted due to Sunday engineering work at Box. No 1940 was built in 1966, later renumbered 47497, then 47717 and named *Tayside Region* between 1988 and 1990, but now de-named and painted in Parcels Sector red livery.

The curve was taken out of use in March 1990 and the track subsequently lifted. In the background an 'Express Sprinter' Class '158' DMU is glimpsed on the Bathampton to Westbury line operating as the 06.30 Cardiff to Portsmouth train on 13 June 1994. *J. H. Sparkes/GR*

BRADFORD-ON-AVON is a picturesque stone-built town on the River Avon, spanned by an old bridge with a tiny lock-up jail on it, with steep alleyways and a Saxon church. To compliment this there is an attractive railway station appropriately designed by Brunel's assistants in a handsome 'Gothic' style built in the local Bath stone. In this view looking east towards Bradford Junctions, the plate steel and corrugated-iron-roofed footbridge is prominent, and the station is neat and well kept. Note also the GWR porter's trolley and GWR notice-board requesting passengers to cross the line by the footbridge. Having emerged from the 159-yard-long tunnel, 'Modified Hall' No 7924 *Thorneycroft Hall* is arriving with the 1.00 pm all stations Salisbury to Bristol train on 10 August 1963. This locomotive had a short life - built at Swindon in September 1950, it was withdrawn as one of the last survivors of the Class in December 1965.

Bradford is certainly the most attractive and best kept of the ten surviving 'smaller' stations/halts in the county today, no doubt enhanced by the fact that it remains manned and has not been reduced to an unstaffed halt, which sadly in this day and age makes such a place a target for vandalism. The buildings are in good condition and the station even retains its GWR station seats. The only noticeable changes are the removal of the footbridge roof and the less tidy state of the shrubs and platform garden, but the whole scene makes a pleasing setting with No 37425 *Sir Robert McAlpine/Concrete Bob* arriving with the 16.30 Weymouth to Bristol train on 3 July 1993. This locomotive was built by English Electric/Vulcan Foundry in 1965 and is seen in its current livery of two-tone grey and Trainload Construction Sector markings. *Hugh Ballantyne/GR*

53

AVONCLIFF HALT, just over 3 miles from Bradford Junction, is one of the smallest halts still open on the BR network. The Wilts, Somerset & Weymouth Railway line between Bathampton and Bradford Junction, a distance of 8³/₄ miles, was opened as a single broad gauge line on 2 February 1857, but this halt only opened on 9 July 1906 and is situated in a scenic location in the valley of the River Avon. At the western end of the platforms the twin-arched bridge is an aqueduct carrying the Kennet & Avon Canal over the valley, across both railway and river, under which the Beyer Peacock-built 'Hymek' is passing with a train heading towards Trowbridge in October 1968.

Today, fortunately, the halt remains open for business and is well cared for, as is evident in this 4 April 1994 view. The apparent changes are the replacement of the Great Western-style nameboard and the loss of the wooden waiting shelter on the up platform, which was demolished during some gales in 1990. 'Express Sprinters' are now regularly seen on this route, and No 158830 is passing as the 07.39 Milford Haven to Portsmouth Harbour train. *Paul Strong/GR*

FRESHFORD is now the first station open on the line from Bathampton south to Bradford-on-Avon. Opened on 2 February 1857, it is situated in the picturesque Limpley Stoke valley of the River Avon, and continues to serve an attractive, somewhat isolated village away from main roads. This 2 June 1963 picture is looking towards Bathampton, and under the footbridge the signal box can be seen on the up side, beyond which were extensive sidings between here and Limpley Stoke.

All the station buildings on both sides have been demolished, but the original platforms and footbridge, minus awning, remain, as does some of the distinctive wooden fencing on the up platform, so some of the traditional railway atmosphere is retained, appropriate in this case as the elegant VSOE Pullman train comes sedately around the curve on 25 April 1994 returning to Victoria from an outing to Bath. The traction is provided by recently renumbered No 47759, built in 1964 as D1605, later 47028 and 47559 *Sir Joshua Reynolds*, but now unnamed and painted in Rail Express Systems red livery. *C. L. Caddy/GR*

LIMPLEY STOKE was the first station on the line between Bathampton and Bradford, and was situated just inside the Wiltshire county boundary in an attractive setting in the deep valley of the River Avon, which railway, river, road and canal traverse. In consideration of the opening of the branch from Camerton on 9 May 1910 (see opposite) the GWR decided to rebuild Limpley Stoke station, so the platforms were lengthened and a bay platform on the west side of the north end of the station was constructed and new buildings erected. This 22 May 1959 view shows the station looking north long after the Camerton branch had closed and the bay platform been removed. Limpley Stoke station closed completely on 3 October 1966.

By 11 April 1994 the platforms have disappeared, but the former station building on the down platform remains as a PW hut and today's train is photographed as closely as possible to the 'past' scene, despite the loss of the platform. 'Express Sprinter' No 158824 is seen coming round the curve working as the 15.45 Cardiff to Portsmouth service. *Colin G. Maggs/GR*

LIMPLEY STOKE (CAMERTON BRANCH): The rural branch line which went from Limpley Stoke to Camerton and Hallatrow ran parallel to the main line towards Bathampton from the actual junction at Limpley Stoke station for 700 yards before turning westwards at an 11-chain radius on an embankment to cross the Midford Brook and county boundary just behind the photographer of this picture. It then passed under the bridge seen here, which carries the A36 Bath to Warminster Road over the line and, to the left, across the viaduct over the Midford Brook and valley floor, while the road on the left is the B3108 from Bradford-on-Avon. The branch was built by the well-known contractors Pauling & Co Ltd, whose founder, George Pauling, had been associated with Cecil Rhodes in Africa in constructing much of the Cape to Cairo railway, particularly in what later became Rhodesia.

At this point the branch took the course of the former Somersetshire Coal Canal and was opened, without ceremony, with a railmotor service of five trains a day on 9 May 1910. As an economy measure during the First World War passenger services were withdrawn on 22 March 1915, but were reinstated, long after the war, on 9 July 1923. This proved to be very short-lived, as the branch was not viable against bus competition and passenger services ceased again, this time finally, on 21 September 1925. Daily coal trains ran to Camerton until the colliery there closed in April 1950, and the surviving goods trains between Monkton Combe and Limpley Stoke ceased on 15 February 1951, when 'Dean Goods' No 2444 hauled the last train. Even then the branch refused to die, as during the summer of 1952 the classic Ealing comedy *The Titfield Thunderbolt* was mainly filmed on the branch, which saw '14XX' Class 0-4-2Ts Nos 1401 and 1456 supporting the renovated 1838-built 0-4-2 *Lion* as the 'star' of the film. After this excitement the track lay dormant, as seen here on 4 October 1956, until it was lifted during 1958.

The trackbed between this point and Monkton Combe provides an access road to commercial premises and a mill at Monkton Combe, so today one can drive under the bridge once traversed by '14XXs' and 'Dean Goods' amongst others. To the right a new access has been formed to a boatyard on what had been the Somersetshire Coal Canal Wharf at the point near where it meets the Kennet & Avon Canal. Although useful as access, no attempt has been made to tidy up the site, and it presents something of an eyesore in an otherwise beautiful setting. *J. Spencer Gilks/GR*

TROWBRIDGE (1), despite being Wiltshire's administrative county town, never seems to have received the attention it perhaps deserves from railway historians/photographers. Originally on the Wilts, Somerset & Weymouth Railway, opened on 5 September 1848, it became a very busy junction station. When this picture was taken, on 5 November 1974, Class '50' No 50024 (subsequently named *Vanguard*) was passing through non-stop with the diverted 11.45 Weston-super-Mare to Paddington train. This locomotive was built by English Electric in 1968 and withdrawn in February 1991.

The station remains open for passenger traffic, but its once important goods yard, extensive sidings and engine shed, all situated behind the station buildings and footbridge in the 'past' view, have gone, goods traffic having ceased on 10 July 1967. Also the attractive station buildings have been demolished and replaced with more austere facilities, the footbridge has been replaced, and the up platform on the left shortened. No 47781, looking smart in Rail Express Systems livery, is passing through with a VSOE special outing to Bath and Bristol returning to Victoria on 17 June 1994. *J. H. Sparkes/GR*

TROWBRIDGE (2): This picture was taken just south of the station on 4 May 1963 and is a good example of an attractive Western Region train of the period. No 7925 *Westol Hall* is hauling a rake of Mark I BR coaches forming the 10.30 Cardiff-Portsmouth train; the leading coach is in Western Region 'chocolate and cream' livery and the remainder maroon. No 7925 looks very smart in its lined green livery as it pulls away towards the next stop at Westbury; however, it was withdrawn in December 1965.

The scene on 22 December 1993 shows how redevelopment has taken place; the modern low-level flats occupying what had been garden ground to the right and a new road bridge for the link road between the town centre and Westbury Road cannot compare in architectural and visual terms to the WS&WR standard bridge built in hard limestone with a soffit profile. The photographer was indeed pleased to see the 09.00 Bristol-Southampton holiday relief short-dated train hauled by No 37407 *Loch Long*, albeit somewhat grubby in main-line livery, rather than the usual Class '156' or '158' DMU trains that nowadays dominate the services. *M. Mensing/GR*

HAWKERIDGE JUNCTION was situated just north of Westbury on the Trowbridge line, and the signal box was built in 1942 to control the junction of the chord line round to the Berks & Hants main line near Heywood Road Junction. Very grubby looking Standard Class '5' No 73020 heads north towards Trowbridge with the 11.05 (SO) Weymouth to Wolverhampton train on 14 August 1965. At the time Class '5s', of either BR Standard or LMS Stanier designs, were frequently diagrammed for this summer train.

On 17 June 1994 the track layout remains that of a traditional double track arrangement and has not been reduced to a 'ladder' junction, as recently renumbered No 47781 comes on to the points with the prestigious VSOE Pullman making a day tour from Victoria to Bath and Bristol. Although the signal box and signals were removed in 1984, the three prominent telegraph poles remain visible above the train in each picture. *Hugh Ballantyne/GR*

Westbury and the GWR to Salisbury

WESTBURY (1): In 1845 the Wilts, Somerset & Weymouth Railway was authorised to build a broad gauge railway from Thingley, west of Chippenham, to Salisbury, with branches to Weymouth, Devizes, Bradford and Bridport. I. K. Brunel was appointed Engineer, and work commenced immediately towards Westbury, Bruton and Salisbury. On 5 September 1848 the railway from Thingley Junction to Westbury, 13 miles 54 chains in length, was opened, and the fine undated old print below shows the original Westbury station designed by J. Geddes, one of Brunel's Principal Assistants. It was built of timber and, as can be seen, had an overall roof. To the right, on the north-west side of the railway, the blast furnace of the Westbury Iron Works can be made out.

That original station was demolished during 1899 and replaced by the facility seen above right, which was opened in April 1900 with two substantial island platforms 600 feet long. With track and junction layouts altered, it greatly improved the amenities at this important railway junction. Access to the platforms was, and still is, from the entrance building on the extreme left via a subway under the platforms. On the right a '517' Class 0-4-2T is shunting coaching stock, while in the background the ironworks continue to dominate the scene. These works came into use in about 1856 using locally excavated ore and also that from north of Bristol. The ironstone workings around Westbury were extensive, connected to the smelting works by 2-foot-gauge railways. Although smelting ceased in 1908, the works continued in use until 1923.

There is a time span of approximately 90 years between the previous picture and this one, dated 4 February 1994 (below right), so, not surprisingly, substantial changes have taken place. The ironworks disappeared in the 1920s and no trace of it remains today; industrial development has taken place on the site, as seen to the right of this picture. From the railway point of view the greatest changes did not take place until 1984, when the station was closed completely between 7 April and 13 May to allow comprehensive remodelling of the north-end layout and signalling to take place. On 14 May 1984 the new Westbury Power Box took control of the much-simplified track layout over which No 37422 *Robert F. Fairlie* is seen departing with the 10.15 ECS working to Cardiff. *Courtesy of D. Walden (2)/GR*

WESTBURY (2): The impressive layout and array of signals can be seen here at the north end of Westbury station on a fine summer's evening in June 1967. An unidentified 'Western' Class diesel-hydraulic pulls out of the station past Westbury North signal box with the 2.00 pm Penzance to Paddington express. On the right is another diesel-hydraulic, one of the smaller 'Warship' series, and to the right of this engine are the lines leading to the diesel depot and yard.

Despite the loss of the signal box and signals, at least the station's island platforms with their fine awnings remain virtually intact. Also, the occasional locomotive-hauled passenger train obligingly passes by, in this instance No 37422 *Robert F. Fairlie* leaving with the 16.30 Weymouth to Bristol on 18 June 1994, the whole ensemble looking very smart in Regional Railways livery. *G. F. Heiron/GR*

WESTBURY SHED provided power for a wide range of semi-fast and local passenger duties together with goods and many shunting/trip workings in the area, requiring no less an allocation than 71 locomotives in December 1947. Opened in 1915 and closed in September 1965, the shed contained four straight roads with a repair shop on the right-hand side. In this 23 May 1929 view the engines are (from left to right) Nos 5536, 6307 and 3384. The latter, a 'Bulldog', was built in September 1903 as No 3446 and named *Swindon*; eventually renumbered 3384, it lost its name in May 1927, some say to avoid confusion with train destinations, and was withdrawn in May 1936.

No trace remains on 13 June 1994; the site, still owned by BR, has been cleared and levelled and is open unused ground, just part of a large tract of BR land at Westbury. *H. C. Casserley/GR*

DILTON MARSH HALT (1): Two miles south-west of Westbury is the village of Dilton Marsh were the Salisbury line of the Great Western makes a stiff climb southwards towards Upton Scudamore for $2^{1}/_{2}$ miles at 1 in 70/75. Approximately halfway up this incline is Dilton Marsh Halt, unstaffed and made of staggered timber platforms and waiting shelters. The halt was opened on 1 June 1937, 81 years after the railway to Salisbury saw its first train. Until BR introduced Conductor/Guards on its diesel multiple units, tickets were bought by intending passengers at 'Holmdale'. The notice advising this unique fact and the location of the ticket office is seen here on the bridge abutment below the halt on 12 July 1969.

The halt remains open for passenger traffic, but tickets are no longer bought before you join the train. The reduced-size noticeboard now surprisingly only shows local bus route services, and BR dos not even bother to show the times of its own railway services on the empty right-hand side of the board. A modern 'footpath to station' sign advises intending passengers of the route to the platform, and Swindon influence still prevails in that the cast iron gateposts, square with sunken panels and ball top, and the pedestrian gate with the standard spearhead railings, all Swindon-made, still perform on 6 December 1993 the job they were designed for. *Hugh Ballantyne/GR*

DILTON MARSH HALT (2): This platform-level view looking towards Westbury shows the timber platform of the up-side staggered platforms as 'Castle' Class No 5005 *Manorbier Castle* climbs the 1 in 75 gradient with a Cardiff to Portsmouth train on 2 July 1955. This locomotive, built at Swindon in June 1928 and withdrawn in June 1960, was one of two engines that the GWR decided to partially 'streamline' in 1935, as was fashionable at the time, and its appearance, together with 'King' Class No 6014, was considerably altered with coverings and a 'bullet nose' on the smokebox front end. These fittings were removed gradually, and by 1946 the 'Castle' had reverted to a normal appearance.

The halt was closed between 5 March and 30 April 1994 for the rebuilding of the shortened platforms, which still remain staggered on each side of the line. On reopening, a plaque was unveiled by the late Sir John Betjeman's daughter Candida Lycett Green commemorating both the rebuilding and the poem 'Dilton Marsh Halt' written by the former Poet Laureate. In this 17 February 1994 scene, taken just before the temporary closing, American-built General Motors Class '59/1' No 59101 *Village of Whatley*, owned by ARC Ltd, comes up grade with its roadstone train from Whatley Quarry heading towards Eastleigh. *R. E. Toop/GR*

WARMINSTER was the first station on the Great Western line from Westbury to Salisbury, 5 miles to the south-east at the top of the stiff climb past Dilton Marsh Halt on varying gradients around 1 in 70; the line was opened to Warminster on 9 September 1851, but it was another five years before trains reached Salisbury. From here it is downhill through the Wylye valley until the railway meets up with the Southern at Wilton. Warminster station had wooden buildings and a standard-style footbridge with ornate latticework sides, decorative valancing and a galvanised corrugated iron canopy, as seen here in this 29 April 1928 view looking south towards Salisbury.

Surprisingly in this age, the station still retains its wooden building on the up side and its footbridge, albeit with canopy removed, a crossover and one up siding. The goods yard has gone but the station remains in business, as seen here on 29 March 1994, with passengers having disembarked from 'Express' DMU No 158822, which is just pulling away as the 14.30 Cardiff General to Portsmouth Harbour train. *H. C. Casserley/GR*

HEYTESBURY: From Warminster the GWR's Salisbury line turned south-east to follow the Wylye valley and, after crossing the river of that name, came to this first station at Heytesbury. It was opened to passenger traffic with the other intermediate stations on 30 June 1856, but missed its centenary by one year. This 17 September 1955 photograph was taken on the last day of service and shows the penultimate down train, the 4.32 pm Bristol to Portsmouth, hauled by No 5904 *Kelham Hall*, drawing away towards Salisbury.

On 6 December 1993 the station building on the down side remains disused and the steel plate minor road overbridge is unaltered. There are now no intermediate stops for any trains between Warminster and Salisbury, a distance of 19¹/₂ miles. *Hugh Ballantyne/GR*

CODFORD, looking from the west end towards Salisbury on 17 September 1955, shows the Great Western style of country station with small standard-type brick and timber signal box and steel plate, corrugated-iron-roofed footbridge. The down siding trailing in in the centre foreground at one time connected to a military branch to Codford Camp, which was built during the First World War in 1914 and operated until 1923. South Wiltshire was noted for a large number of military camps and training areas, and indeed today Tidworth in the south-east remains an important military base. This station, together with the other intermediate ones between Warminster and Salisbury, was a relatively early victim of BR's closure plans, and this picture shows the very last up train to stop here. No 5080 *Defiant* is piloting No 4968 *Shotton Hall* as they pause with the 5.02 pm Salisbury to Cardiff train. Nine passengers alighted from the train at 5.30 pm with no outward sign of interest or emotion as this little station quietly passed into history.

There was no evidence on 6 December 1993 that there had once been a station here, just an automatic barrier crossing protecting the minor road in place of the signal box and crossing gates. *Hugh Ballantyne/GR*

WYLYE on 15 September 1936 presents a scene of complete orderliness in that timeless era when the railway was the major means of transportation for goods and passengers throughout the kingdom. In this picture, looking south-east towards Salisbury, note the tidy station layout on and off the platforms, the trimmed bushes on the up side and the substantial goods shed - from its generous arch you can clearly see that it was built for broad gauge track, but in fact this line was converted to 'narrow' (standard) gauge on 19 June 1874 after only 18 years on the 7 ft 0¼ in gauge.

Another depressing modern contrast! On 18 April 1994 all of the neat station has gone, to be replaced by uncontrolled vegetation and wild scrub. The level crossing for the minor road to Dinton now has automatic barriers and both signal box and good shed have disappeared as two single Class '121' units, built by Pressed Steel Limited in 1960, coupled together for use as route-learning vehicles, head towards Salisbury. Both units remain in Network SouthEast livery, and the nearest, L130, was formerly No 55020. *H. C. Casserley/GR*

Past and Present
Colour

Wiltshire

HIGHWORTH: The little market town of Highworth lies some 6 miles to the north-east of Swindon. The railway was promoted by the Swindon & Highworth Light Railway, but like so many Victorian railway enterprises, it failed before it was able to complete its line to the satisfaction of the Board of Trade Inspecting Officer, so it fell into the hands of the Great Western and was opened to public traffic on 9 May 1883. This was the terminus station of the branch, $5^1/_2$ miles from the main-line junction and situated on a rising gradient of 1 in 203, at the top of an even sharper rise of half a mile at 1 in 44. This picture shows part of the simple wooden station building, goods shed and diamond-pattern blue brick platform paving as Class '03' D2195 climbs into the station with the unadvertised evening workmen's train, the 5.28 pm from Swindon, on 18 June 1962, six weeks before closure.

By April 1994 all trace of the station has gone, and the area now forms a residential area known as Home Farm Estate. This photograph is as near an approximation as possible to the 'past' picture. *Hugh Ballantyne/Graham Roose*

SWINDON STOCK SHED, on the north-east side of the vast Swindon railway complex, was situated near the locomotive depot adjacent to the line to Kemble. It was designed for storing motive power and rolling-stock, although
in later days it was used for holding engines awaiting a decision or scrapping. When this picture of No 1003 *County
of Dorset* was taken on 20 September 1964 the locomotive had been withdrawn for two months, hence its sad
appearance without nameplates, numberplates or connecting rods. The Dynamometer Car, No W7W, had been built
at Swindon in 1907 for use in road-resting locomotives to measure their effectiveness as power units. The car was
used in the well-known Locomotive Exchanges of 1948, but in 1961, when a replacement was built, W7W was
retired. It is seen here stored out of use pending scrapping, but fortuitously it was subsequently saved for preservation and is now safely installed on the Dart Valley Railway. Part of the gas works built and owned by the GWR
is visible in the background, with the largest of four gasholders, of 2.5 million cu ft capacity, prominent. This works
was closed in January 1959 and supplies subsequently obtained from the South Western Gas Board, who took over
that particular holder.

Development has completely
transformed the locality by April
1994, but the gasholder remains, its
top just visible left of centre, albeit
now storing natural gas rather than
manufactured town gas. *Hugh
Ballantyne/Graham Roose*

MALMESBURY was reached by an independent company that built a line from the GWR main line at Dauntsey, a distance of 6½ miles, which opened on 17 December 1877. Not surprisingly, the company was taken over by the GWR in 1892, and following the opening of the South Wales direct line from Wootton Bassett, the branch connected with that line at Little Somerford, and eventually by 1933 the shortened branch of 3¾ miles came into use, and the section to Dauntsey was closed. As seen here on 12 June 1962, goods traffic continued to thrive and the yard was busy, particularly with loads of farm machinery from Messrs Blanch, so much so that implements were parked on the station platform for loading. Class '03' diesel shunter D2187 is seen at work shunting past the station platform. The attractive Cotswold-stone-built station is still complete with its canopy, although the bay windows are boarded up. On the left the small single-road engine shed, closed in 1951, has lost the track leading to it.

While one would expect that the splendid but partly ruined Abbey church, clearly visible in both pictures, would continue to dominate the landscape, surprisingly the little loco shed also survives in February 1994, albeit reno-

vated and with the ends filled in, and now serving as part of a small tyre-fitting business. The trackbed, station and goods yard have all been swallowed up by redevelopment as an industrial estate, and a mature tree has grown up in the position once occupied by D2187.
Hugh Ballantyne/Graham Roose

HOLT JUNCTION station was unusual in Wiltshire, being a small country station comprising an island platform only. It was also in an isolated location some way from the nearest habitation. The railway from Thingley Junction was opened in 1848, but it was not until the line to Devizes was completed in 1857, making its junction here, that a station was constructed, which opened with the Devizes branch on 1 July 1857. It was simply an interchange station with no access to or from the village, unless one walked for a mile across the fields. Eventually in the 1870s a road was made and a goods shed constructed, so the station was then able properly to serve local needs, albeit that passenger access to the platform was by means of a footbridge from the north-west side. On a warm summer's day, 10 August 1963, No 6968 *Woodcock Hall* arrives at the station with a holiday train, the Saturdays-only 11.10 am from Wolverhampton to Weymouth. The station was closed to all traffic on 18 April 1966.

The 11 April 1994 picture was obtained with the permission, help and courtesy of Mr Maurice Arlett, who pinpointed the 'past' location, as little now remains to make identification possible. However, with the aid of tall stepladders placed near the old station approach road where the footbridge had been, and the grass bank on the right forming the rubble/spoil of the demolished island platform, this photograph makes the nearest possible comparison. The surviving running line is that on the left of the 'past' picture. *Hugh Ballantyne/Graham Roose*

WESTBURY: A BR scene on 12 April 1982, when corporate blue for locomotives and blue-grey coaching stock liveries were de rigueur, and no exceptions to the rule tolerated. Even that dreary livery era has now become part of history, and this picture, taken only 12 years before the 'present' equivalent, can now never be repeated. Locomotive-hauled trains no longer operate Portsmouth to Cardiff services such as that seen here behind No 33048, and the semaphore signals and box were superseded by multiple-aspect signalling (MAS) on 14 May 1984. Westbury North box, with 99 levers, controlled the starting signals seen here, and the road is set as No 33048 pulls away from the platform; the distants belong to Hawkeridge Junction.

Nowadays the station, much rationalised trackwise and controlled by MAS, sees very few locomotive-hauled passenger trains. The scene today will produce Class '150' 'Sprinter' DMUs, such as seen here on 18 May 1994 in the form of No 150249 arriving as the 14.20 Swansea-Portsmouth Harbour. Westbury North signal box was demolished in May 1984. *Both Graham Roose*

FAIRWOOD JUNCTION, WESTBURY: This early BR diesel era scene shows blue-liveried 'Hymek' No D7033 passing the junction signal box and taking the Westbury station line with an up stone train comprising 21-ton capacity HOP wagons from Somerset Stone Quarries sidings on 12 July 1969. The signal box here was opened on 1 January 1933 when the Westbury avoiding line, seen in the foreground, came into use, forming one of the well-known GWR 'cut-off' lines built to provide faster through running to its principal destinations, in this case for services to the South West of England. D7033 was a 1,700 hp diesel-hydraulic built for the Western Region by Beyer Peacock in May 1962, but had a very short working life of less than ten years, being withdrawn in January 1972.

It is pleasing to be able to record one of BR's success stories, the introduction of company trains to haul block loads. This complete train, locomotive and bogie stone wagons, is owned by ARC Ltd and painted in that company's livery, and is seen also taking the Westbury line with a load of roadstone from Whatley Quarry, North Somerset. The locomotive, No 59102 *Village of Chantry*, is a 1990-built General Motors 3,300 hp diesel-electric, one of four owned by ARC. Although the track layout remains the same as in the 1969 picture, the signals and box have gone; the latter was closed on 11 May 1984 when the MAS came into operation. *Hugh Ballantyne/Graham Roose*

WILTON SOUTH: Under clear signals from the down starter, with its tall post and repeater arm for sighting purposes, No 34091 *Weymouth* pulls away with the 11.15 (Sundays) all-stations Salisbury to Yeovil Junction local train on 23 June 1963. Just beyond the down sidings can be seen the bridge over the A36 Warminster Road.

No trace of the down platform or sidings remains, although the running lines are still, for a short distance, double track; the single-line section starts round the bend that the Class '159' unit is approaching as it passes by as the 16.30 Salisbury to Gillingham service on 18 April 1994. *Hugh Ballantyne/Graham Roose*

SALISBURY (SR) SHED lay to the west of Salisbury station, and was built by the LSWR as a substantial ten-road shed with its entrance facing east. It was an important shed in the Western Division of the Southern Railway and remained so in BR days, save that it was coded 72B, placing it in the Exmouth Junction (Exeter) group. The shed remained in use to the end of Southern Region steam, closing on 9 July 1967. When this picture was taken on 23 June 1963, except for the diesel shunter all the engines visible were Southern; left to right, they are Nos 35004 *Cunard White Star* and 'S15' No 30512 in the shed, while outside, tender leading, is No 34091 *Weymouth* with 'N' No 31813.

The shed was demolished in November 1969 and the cleared site remains an undeveloped wasteland overgrown with bushes and scrub. No remains of the buildings are visible on 21 February 1994. *Hugh Ballantyne/Graham Roose*

WISHFORD station served the village of Great Wishford, but was always known simply as Wishford. It was close by its village, at which point the railway curved more to the south for a further 2 miles towards Wilton where the rivers Nadder and Wylye meet. Coming round into the station on a particularly wet 2 September 1955, No 5946 *Marwell Hall* is slowing for a brief stop while working the 5.02 pm Salisbury to Cardiff train.

It proved impossible to find a platform-level comparison picture as no trace of the station remains and the line is well fenced at this point. However, due to the kindness of the owner of the Station House, this picture was taken from a bedroom window on 18 April 1994 and shows an 'Express' Class '158' unit coming round the curve working as the 14.20 Portsmouth Harbour to Cardiff General service. In the background the wooded ridge of Grovely Hill, rising to 450 feet, is prominent, beyond which is the valley of the River Nadder and the Southern line from Exeter. *Hugh Ballantyne/GR*

QUIDHAMPTON: This location, which never had a station, was a village between Salisbury and Wilton, and this 27 August 1963 picture shows a train heading towards Wilton with the western suburbs of Salisbury just behind the train; the two tracks here were the 1856 Great Western lines from Westbury to Salisbury. An unidentified 'Hymek' diesel-hydraulic is hauling a Bristol-bound train, judging by its length probably a through dated summer service from the South Coast.

The usual present-day scene shows a mass of wild vegetation and scrub obliterating much of the lineside and the single line of the headshunt for what is now the English China Clay siding ending at the buffer-stop. Housing development on the edge of Salisbury has extended, but at least the ugly and rather short electricity pylon has not been replaced by an even larger or uglier monstrosity! 16 February 1993. *R. A. Lissenden/GR*

West of England main line

LITTLE BEDWYN: The main line of the former Great Western Railway forming part of the direct route from Reading to Taunton was, in this part of Wiltshire, originally built as the Berks & Hants Extension Railway, a single-line broad gauge railway between Hungerford and Devizes opened on 11 November 1862. Later, with the policy of building 'cut-offs', the Great Western was able to shorten a number of its main lines on important traffic routes. Not least was the desire to get its direct route to Devon and Cornwall, and this was partly achieved in Wiltshire by the opening of the 14 miles 35 chains of line between Patney & Chirton and Westbury, to goods traffic on 29 July and to passengers from 1 October 1900.

On the Berks & Hants line (clearly misnamed, as the Extension line passed from Berkshire into Wiltshire without touching Hampshire) the first place of interest in the county was just south-west of Hungerford where the railway closely paralleled the Kennet & Avon Canal at Little Bedwyn. There was never a station here, but the railway passed by the tiny village between the church and locks of the canal. In a classic Great Western setting No 6026 *King John* passes with the down 'Cornish Riviera', the 10.30 Paddington to Penzance express on 24 June 1956.

Something of an improvement is evident in the scene on 6 April 1994 - as is well known the Kennet & Avon Canal has been painstakingly restored and the lock is now operational after many years of disuse. The canal side has also been tidied up and landscaped and fortunately, except for the unnecessarily large fence between the line and canal, and the tree protruding into the left side of the picture, the location still enables a very pleasing photograph of canal and train to be obtained. Let us hope that neither BR nor the Canal Trust seek to spoil the scene by planting trees or bushes along the fence, thus restricting the sight of this down HST working as the 14.25 Paddington to Penzance service. *E. W. Fry/GR*

BEDWYN was, and still is, the first station in Wiltshire on the main line from Paddington to Westbury. It was opened on 11 November 1862 and serves the delightful village of Great Bedwyn situated on the south-east side of Savernake Forest. This 24 February 1965 picture, looking south-west towards Westbury, shows the simple layout with the tiny Elizabethan-styled stone-built station building on the up platform and a wooden waiting shelter on the down side. Trains that called here were services that ran via Devizes rather than direct on the main line to and from Westbury. Goods facilities were withdrawn on 7 September 1964.

The station remains open for passengers; indeed, it is included in the Network SouthEast commuter service to Paddington and therefore enjoys some direct trains to London in peak hours with a reasonable service throughout the day, albeit with a change at Reading. It is an attractive station, save that the station building has been demolished, and, typical of today's unstaffed halts, all that is offered for waiting passengers is a modern 'bus shelter' structure, which can be seen by the car park in this 6 April 1994 view. The down shelter remains and the platform surfaces and lighting have been restyled. The non-stopping HST on the up line is the 13.35 Plymouth to Paddington train. *C. L. Caddy/GR*

CROFTON was where the railway and Kennet & Avon Canal were near their respective summits as they curved westwards beyond Bedwyn in order to overcome the high ground of Savernake Forest. The canal, opened in 1810, was 400 feet above sea level at its summit at Savernake, and to harmonise the water levels 106 locks had to be constructed, of which there were no fewer than 31 between Savernake and Newbury. By necessity, Crofton Pumping Station was constructed to pump the water and it stands prominently on the north side of the track as No 6017 *King Edward IV* comes round the curve on the rising 1 in 175 gradient with the down 'Royal Duchy', the 1.30 pm Paddington to Penzance express, on 25 March 1958.

The pumping station chimney has been shortened, but otherwise the buildings remain. Fortunately this picture was taken before the spring growth developed so one is able to see more clearly and compare the features as an HST working the 12.35 Paddington to Penzance as it comes round the curve on 6 April 1994. This comparison substantiates the case for the campaign to tidy up the railway linesides! *R. C. Riley/GR*

WOLFHALL JUNCTION: The train coming off the Midland & South Western Junction Railway on 20 March 1959, the 2.50 pm Andover Junction to Swindon Junction hauled by Pannier tank No 3666, is approaching Great Western track at Wolfhall Junction situated three-quarters of a mile east of Savernake Low Level station. The main line looking east towards Newbury curves away under the 74-foot-span girder bridge that carries the M&SWJR's direct route to Savernake High Level and northwards to Marlborough.

While the course of the old M&SWJR route is recognisable on 6 April 1994, Wolfhall Junction signal box, the girder overbridge and all track except the Berks & Hants line has been removed. The HST on the up main line is the 09.42 Penzance to Paddington train. *J. Spencer Gilks/GR*

SAVERNAKE LOW LEVEL, on the Berks & Hants Extension Railway, was opened in 1862, and was situated at the summit of a long steady climb of over 30 miles eastwards from Theale, after which the line descends for 18 miles to Lavington. This picture was taken in the summer of 1960 from the road overbridge at the west end of the platforms and shows the track layouts and junction, with a Pannier tank arriving off the branch from Marlborough and running into the bay platform used by those trains. To the right of the main line is Savernake West signal box, behind which its up home and the Savernake East intermediate distant are both off, so an up train is approaching. Quite unseen, immediately underneath the railway at this point is the 500-yard-long Bruce Tunnel of the Kennet &

Avon Canal, this, like the station, being at the Canal summit. The station closed to goods traffic in May 1964 and to passengers on 18 April 1966.

Station, junction track layout and signals have gone, but still unseen the canal tunnel under the railway remains, as does the double track of the West of England main line. The approaching HST on 23 June 1994 is the 13.35 Plymouth to Paddington. Visible links with the past are the fence posts on top of the cutting and one of the poles, also on the top. *Roderick Hoyle/GR*

BURBAGE WHARF: As we have seen, the Berks & Hants Extension Railway closely followed the course of the Kennet & Avon Canal for about 10 miles between Hungerford and Wootton Rivers. Shortly after the railway opened in 1862, a siding and goods shed was provided at a wharf alongside the canal. This was a somewhat unusual occurrence of co-operation between railway and canal, as the latter were hostile in the early days of railways because of the competition that they generated. Although contemplated during construction of the railway, no passenger station was provided; it was decided to locate the station 1 mile to the east at Savernake, the line summit. Only one siding was laid into a goods shed with access at both ends to the up main line and a short siding serving some cattle pens, once located to the right of the locomotive in this picture. Burbage Siding signal box stood on the down side and a trailing crossover from down to up side gave access from the down line to the siding. The canal is not visible from this angle, taken from the main road overbridge, but is parallel to the railway to the right of the goods shed. The goods station was closed on 10 November 1947 and the siding and signal box subsequently removed. No doubt the fireman was earning his keep on No 5986 *Arbury Hall*, seen in lined black livery, as the Weymouth to Paddington express comes past the old goods shed on 21 May 1956 and nears the top of more or less 15 miles of steady climb from Lavington.

This HST will have made light work of the same length of up grade as it speeds towards Reading and Paddington as the 08.47 from Penzance on 6 April 1994. This is the up 'Cornish Riviera' according to the timetable, but other than sticky labels on the doors of the coaches no one could possibly differentiate this train from any other of the dozens of daily HST services on the railway. More vegetation is now evident and hides the field of the 'past' picture, in which a very old-looking lorry appeared to be parked as a feed store or hay barn. Perhaps some enthusiast has now saved and restored it as another valuable relic of our past heritage? *E. W. Fry/GR*

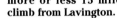

PEWSEY: Of the attractive wayside stations constructed on the Berks & Hants Extension Railway, this was the largest in Wiltshire, built in a soft-pink-coloured brick in Elizabethan style. This 29 September 1962 view shows the building on the down side and a neat wooden shelter facing opposite to serve the up platform. A three-car DMU approaches the platform, working as the 11.05 Westbury to Newbury train.

The station remains open for passengers and, most surprisingly, the up platform now boasts a waiting room constructed in an architectural style compatible with the existing station, to replace the wooden shelter. This perfectly compliments the original building still remaining, albeit with chimney stacks removed, but the goods shed, signal box and crossover have gone. The approaching HST is the up 'Cornish Riviera', the 08.47 Penzance to Paddington, on 31 January 1994. *Colin G. Maggs/GR*

WOODBOROUGH station conveniently served its village and this fine picture shows just how attractive the rural railway stations of England could be. This example shows a very small station building in a neat Elizabethan style partly hidden by the even smaller timber building on the down side. The goods shed beyond clearly shows that the rail-side opening was wide enough to accommodate broad gauge track, as a down train passes *en route* towards Westbury on 29 September 1962. On the north side beyond the signal box was an up loop and one siding; note the Austin 8 saloon parked alongside the box. The station closed to passengers on 18 April 1966 and to goods traffic four months later.

The entire infrastructure visible in the 'past' picture has disappeared. There is at least a down loop, considerably longer than the siding in the 1962 scene, and a trailing crossover that the 09.35 Plymouth to Paddington is about to pass on 31 January 1994. Fortunately the area is not overgrown with vegetation, but now has ugly huts on the up side and a little brick building and telecommunications mast on the down. Railway fencing and retaining wall remain evident on the right. *Colin G. Maggs/GR*

PATNEY & CHIRTON: As a first step to improving the line from Paddington to Taunton, the Berks & Hants Extension from Hungerford was doubled as far as what became Patney & Chirton station as the Great Western set about constructing its 'new route to the West' in the latter years of the last century. A new line to Westbury was also constructed, and this new station was opened for passengers with the Westbury line on 1 October 1900. The station had three platforms, the one on the left forming an island for the up main line and, on its outer edge, for local trains to and from Devizes. Looking east, the photographer is standing with the signal box and down main starter immediately behind him as an immaculate 'Castle' Class engine races through the station with the down 'Torbay Express' from Paddington to Kingswear in March 1958. To the left of the locomotive are the starter bracket signals for trains from the outer edge of the island to either the Devizes branch or crossing over to the down main line.

The substantial steel plate footbridge survives, but no longer echoes to the tread of passengers crossing to or from the island platform, being retained for the other part of its requirement which is to permit access, then as now, from one side of the railway to the other. The station was closed to goods traffic in May 1964 and passengers on 18 April 1966, and on 8 November 1993 the footbridge is the only reminder of this pleasant rural GWR junction station. *Paul Strong/GR*

LAVINGTON was one of the two stations on the 'cut-off' line from Patney & Chirton to Westbury, 81 miles from Paddington. It had all the GWR features of the period when it opened on 1 October 1900, as evidenced by the new type of standard signal box and the plate steel footbridge, seen in this view looking east towards Newbury on 1 May 1966. The station was closed to passengers on 18 April of that year and, nearly a year later, for goods on 3 April 1967.

Today only the main running lines are evident with a scrapyard on the south side in the station approach road and yard. The passing HST is the 'Cornish Riviera', 10.35 Paddington to Penzance, on 30 March 1994. *C. L. Caddy/GR*

EDINGTON & BRATTON was the other station on the 'cut-off' line west of Patney & Chirton, and opened on the same day as Lavington, 1 October 1900. This picture was taken in August 1957 after the platform edging stones had been removed, the station having closed to passengers on 3 November 1952. 'Hall' Class No 4983 *Albert Hall* heads west into the evening sun with down empty milk tanks returning from London to West of England milk depots. The engine was built at Swindon in January 1931 and withdrawn in December 1963.

The steel plate road overbridge, roadside fencing and the pole on the extreme right remain, but other than that there was no trackside evidence of the station on 13 December 1993. *Paul Strong/GR*

FAIRWOOD JUNCTION: Speeding around the curve of the Westbury avoiding line, D1052 'Western Viceroy' heads IB95 from Paddington to the West of England on a summer Saturday, 19 August 1972. The ancient Westbury White Horse is just discernible on the chalk hillside of Bratton Down to the right of the telegraph pole. D1052 was built for the Western Region at Crewe in January 1963, withdrawn in October 1975 and cut up six months later.

The signals and wooden PW hut have gone and the vegetation on the sides of the cutting is worse than ever, thus partly obscuring this view of a down HST working as the 11.35 Paddington to Penzance train on 25 June 1994. *Hugh Ballantyne/GR*

SEEND station was on the Holt Junction to Devizes and Patney & Chirton line; although the line opened on 1 July 1857, this station did not appear in the public timetable until 1858. It was extended with the provision of two platforms, signal box and sidings in about 1906 when a local iron ore mine was revived, and until the mine closed in 1935 and wartime traffic ceased, it was a busy station. On 10 June 1956 the signal box was closed and the platform loop removed, as can be seen in this picture. Access to the remaining sidings was controlled by ground frames operated by the Holt-Devizes electric train token. In this vicinity the branch was quite straight, but the change in gradient upwards from 1 in 123 and 1 in 79 in the Devizes direction is readily apparent. Leaving the station in the down direction is No 5993 *Kirby Hall* on a local train.

The running line trackbed has now become a farm access road and trees and vegetation have gained considerably. However, the minor road overbridge once at the east end of the station remained in use on 17 November 1993. *Paul Strong/GR*

BROMHAM & ROWDE: This halt was opened on 22 February 1909 and appears to have generated much more traffic than originally envisaged. In addition to the then usual corrugated steel sheeted 'Pagoda', a quite substantial awning and a porter's cabin was provided at a later date. This view is looking towards Holt Junction and was taken on 14 February 1965.

The desolate scene on 6 April 1994 shows partial use of the site as an agricultural yard. While the platform is prominent, not surprisingly the somewhat insubstantial railway buildings have disappeared. Note also that the cutting beyond the platform has been filled in, but the bridge parapets are still visible. *C. L. Caddy/GR*

NEAR BROMHAM & ROWDE: Travelling eastwards past Bromham & Rowde Halt, the railway, road and canal had to surmount the hill on the west side of Devizes rising for 2$^1/_2$ miles on gradients varying between 1 in 52 and 1 in 93. Near milepost 87$^1/_2$ the railway crossed the A361 Devizes to Trowbridge road on an acutely angled overbridge, known locally as 'The Fish', an impressive steel structure shaped like the skeleton of a fish with three large ribs stretching across the rails between the girders on each side. This 14 February 1965 view is looking east towards Devizes.

Not only has the steel girder bridge been removed, but also much of the high railway embankment so as to make room for a short section of dual carriageway on the A361. The remains of the embankment can be seen on the left on 6 April 1994, as the eastbound carriageway is the old road, while that for westbound traffic on the right is completely new. *C. L. Caddy/GR*

DEVIZES (1) was another town approached by the railway from opposite directions at different times. In this case the railway from Holt, to the west, opened in July 1857, while that from Hungerford in the east came five years later in November 1862. At one time the station had an overall roof spanning the two main platforms, that on the south forming an island to give the station a third platform. The layout was quite spacious with sidings on both sides of the running lines and goods shed and yard on the north or up side. This picture shows the first of the 'Modified Hall' Class, No 6959 *Peatling Hall* pulling out of the station with the 3.15 from Westbury to Reading train on 21 March 1964. The station was closed to goods traffic on 2 November of that year, and finally to passengers on 18 April 1966.

The tree above the footbridge in the 'past' scene is visible just right of centre in this 1 February 1994 picture, which shows that the railway has completely disappeared and has been replaced by a car park and some rather ugly barrack-like housing blocks. *Hugh Ballantyne/GR*

DEVIZES (2): Looking in the opposite direction, this picture was taken in the goods sidings on the south side of the station platforms and shows the line curving towards Devizes tunnel, 190 yards long, which passes underneath Devizes Castle, shortly after which Pans Lane Halt was reached. This picture shows perfectly the standard loading gauge adopted by the GWR in 1925, plain and functional and held up by a post made from two rails. From rail level to the inside top of the gauge was 11 feet. Note also the gas-lamp, BR 'totem' station nameplate and two standard GWR starter signals protecting the up platform and the north side of the bi-directional island platform.

This end of the station is also part of the car park, but is clearly the same place as the background houses on the higher ground remain in this 13 December 1993 view. That on the right near the tunnel has been modified by the replacement of the ornate bargeboards with those of a plainer type - no doubt easter to paint! *Paul Strong/GR*

DEVIZES TUNNEL: This picture shows the castellated portal of the east end of the tunnel on 16 May 1959, with Devizes Castle visible in the left background. Emerging is 0-6-0PT No 5416 with the 11.02 from Devizes to Patney service, shortly to make its first and only stop on its 5-mile journey, at Pans Lane Halt, which served a suburb of Devizes and a nearby hospital.

Today the eastern entrance to the tunnel is boarded up, perhaps not surprising as the tunnel has been put to good use by the local small-bore rifle club. The castellated facade remains on 6 April 1994, but the trackbed and once well-tended lineside allotments have now reverted to nature with the usual overgrown and unkempt appearance. *J. Spencer Gilks/GR*

South Western main line and branches

PORTON: Passing the edge of Salisbury Plain, the main line of the London & South Western Railway followed the River Bourne towards Salisbury, and Porton was the last intermediate station before reaching the cathedral city. This section of railway from Andover was opened on 1 May 1857, and on a bright March afternoon in 1967, not long before the station closed to passengers on 9 September 1968, Standard Class '5' No 73093 draws away up the 1 in 140 rising gradient with the 16.00 local train from Salisbury to Basingstoke.

It was impossible to replicate the 'past' scene on 24 June 1994 due to development over much of the station yard, which has become a garden and aquatic centre. The station house in the right background of the 1967 view stood approximately between the building on the left and the 'Turbo' Class '159' DMU heading south as the 10.35 Waterloo to Paignton. *A. S. Eaton/GR*

QUIDHAMPTON: Looking westwards from the minor road overbridge at the end nearest to the A36, we see the double-track main line from Salisbury to Exeter and a typical local train of the era from Yeovil Junction to Salisbury galloping along from Wilton towards the end of its journey on 27 August 1963. The train comprises a neat short rake of Bulleid coaches hauled by Maunsell 'U' Class No 31632, which was built at Ashford in 1931. In the background beyond the third pylon can be seen the end of the north side of the cutting and the former GWR tracks converging from behind it.

Other than the fact that all trains from both the Westbury and Exeter routes now traverse these metals, there is hardly any change at all except for the motive power and flat-bottom track having replaced the old traditional bullhead rails. Even the vegetation has received some attention and has been partially trimmed back by BR engineering staff while Class '47' No 47714 comes up the line with the 12.17 Exeter to Waterloo service on 16 February 1993. The whole train looks very smart in its Network SouthEast livery. *R. A. Lissenden/GR*

WILTON: This interesting picture reminds us that the GWR and LSWR took parallel but separate, unconnected lines from Wilton into Salisbury. The LSWR's station was originally on the first part of the Salisbury & Yeovil Railway, which opened in 1859. Looking south-east towards Salisbury, the GWR track from Westbury, opened in 1856, is on the left and the LSWR, later Southern Railway, nearest the camera, with Bulleid 'Light Pacific' No 34086 *219 Squadron* leaning into the curve towards Wilton South station at the head of the 11.30 Brighton to Plymouth train on 3 August 1964. No 34086 was built at Brighton in 1948 and withdrawn in 1966.

Today's scene is deceptive; although the position of the four tracks is identical, there are now only two running lines on the course of the Southern tracks from Salisbury to Wilton, the former GWR lines having ceased to be used in 1973 when Wilton Junction was substituted beyond the bridge seen in the background of this 6 December 1993 view. Network SouthEast Class '159' three-car DMU No 159015, working as the 10.35 Waterloo to Exeter St Davids, approaches Wilton, at which point the Southern line becomes a single track as far as Templecombe. The only other visible difference is the mass of unsightly vegetation covering the sides of the cuttings and the removal of the telegraph poles. *M. Mensing/GR*

WILTON SOUTH (1): This typical scene from the 1950s shows 'West Country' 'Pacific' No 34038 *Lynton* pulling out of the west end of Wilton South station on 26 July 1952 with a three-coach local train from Salisbury to Exeter. The covered footbridge between the up and down platforms and the down loop can both be seen; the latter became well known in 1947 as the siding in which the down 'Devon Belle' relieving engine awaited the arrival of the train from Waterloo. The public timetable showed the Pullman train as making its first stop at Sidmouth Junction, but because of the lack of water troughs on the Southern an engine stop or change was in fact necessary in view of the distance involved. The Operating Department decided on an engine change at this un-publicised location near Salisbury, the stopping point for all other trains. The 'Devon Belle' was short-lived and ceased running in 1954. The station was closed to goods traffic on 6 July 1964 and to passengers from 7 March 1966. No 34038 was built at Brighton in September 1946 and is seen here in an as-built condition with original cab and high tender plating. It was withdrawn in June 1966 and sold to Cashmores, Newport, for scrap.

The scene today shows that this section of the Salisbury-Exeter line still retains double track from Salisbury, but the down sidings have gone together with the down platform and footbridge. Network SouthEast unit No 159022 is working as the 12.35 Waterloo to Exeter service on 6 December 1993. *Les Elsey/GR*

WILTON SOUTH (2): We are now looking westwards from the Salisbury end of the down platform. The station was opened on 2 May 1859 and shows the neat style of building used and the typical small LSWR wooden signal cabin mounted on a brick base. If you compare this photograph with the view on the previous page, you will see that the footbridge has lost its roof and side windows and both the running lines are laid with flat-bottom rails. Despite the fact that the station was in its declining years when photographed on 8 April 1964, it appears well kept and the signalman is busy cleaning the windows of the box.

Today the up-side station buildings remain remarkably intact and are used as a private residence, but the wooden signal box and its base have been removed. Even the station hut further along the platform remains, but there is no evidence of the down-side platform, sidings or footbridge, just waste-ground now fenced off from the running lines. 6 December 1993. *Colin G. Maggs/GR*

NEAR DINTON: Cantering along up the valley of the River Nadder very much in Wiltshire's chalk country, Standard Class '5' No 73162 is about to pass under the B3089 road overbridge before making its stop at Dinton station with the 11.10 Salisbury to Yeovil local train on 13 August 1964.

Thirty years later, on 17 June 1994, the picture speaks for itself - the line has been singled and vegetation has taken over most of the remainder of the railway land. Network SouthEast 'Turbo' unit No 159018 is about to go under the same bridge working as the 09.35 Waterloo to Gillingham (Dorset), but will miss the now closed station at Dinton and its next stop will be Tisbury. *Terry Gough/GR*

DINTON (1): This view was taken from the minor road overbridge that bisected this station, looking towards Salisbury on 12 April 1966 shortly after the station was closed to passenger traffic. D6506 is shunting government traffic from the sidings that serve the depot at Baverstock and the nearly Dinton Depot, and is coming on to the down main line.

Today this section of the Salisbury-Exeter line is single track, and at this location the former down line is the running line; the track on the left, the old up line, is in fact now used as a long siding serving the MOD Chilmark and Baverstock Depots. The extensive down sidings in the 'past' picture have been lifted and nature is reclaiming the land, but on the north side the access point and siding survive, as do the standard type of Southern Railway concrete lineside platelayers' hut and, on the left, the remains of the up platform. Class '159' 'Turbo' No 159017 approaches, working the 08.35 Waterloo to Exeter service on 14 April 1994. *Colin G. Maggs/GR*

DINTON (2): This is the scene in the opposite direction, looking west, as the 11.04 Salisbury to Yeovil Junction service draws out of the station on a fine spring day, 11 May 1964.

The station buildings and attractive hut on the up platform have passed into private ownership and are well cared for, but the down-side platform and the signal box have gone. At least there is the appearance of double track, even if the old up line has been reduced to the status of a military siding. Network SouthEast 'Turbo' No 159002 is approaching as the 09.32 Yeovil Junction to Waterloo service on 14 April 1994. *H. C. Casserley/GR*

TISBURY: This attractive village was served by the third station west of Salisbury on the Exeter line when it opened as far as Gillingham on 2 May 1859. There were sidings at the west end and a goods yard on the north side of the double-track main line. In this study, looking west, 'S15' Class No 30825 swings out of the yard on to the up main line watched by staff during shunting work on 21 August 1958. The typical wooden LSWR signal box controlling all the operations is to the right of the locomotive and was replaced with a modern structure in October 1958, three months after this photograph was taken.

After the Salisbury-Exeter line fell under the control of the Western Region, rationalisation became the policy, which meant reduction in train services and

102

singling of sections of the route in April 1967. At the Wiltshire end the line was singled at Wilton, and here is the evidence with only the old up line now in use as 'Turbo' unit No 159008 leaves the station working the 09.35 Waterloo to Exeter service on 14 April 1994. All the sidings have gone, but the replacement signal box of 1958 still stands. The land up to the edge of the old down platform on the left is now owned and used by Parmiters, manufacturers of farm machinery, who kindly granted permission for access to take this photograph. Tisbury station remains open for passenger traffic and the majority of trains between Salisbury and Exeter stop here today. *Hugh Ballantyne/GR*

TISBURY GATES: A mile to the west of Tisbury station a minor road drops down into the valley of the little River Sem to bridge the river and immediately make a level crossing with the railway. In the railway's heyday the crossing was protected by semaphore signals, and a crossing-keeper's hut was provided on the up (north) side of the double-track main line. On a dull 21 August 1956 Bulleid 'Pacific' No 34076 *41 Squadron* comes past the Gates working the 6.15 am Plymouth to Salisbury train. The locomotive was built at Brighton in June 1948 and withdrawn in January 1966.

Nowadays the line is singled, the semaphores have gone and the road crossing is an automatic barrier, but the railway house visible on the left remains, as does the attractive wooden crossing-keeper's hut. 22 February 1993. *Hugh Ballantyne/GR*

SEMLEY station was very close to the Dorset border and about a mile from the small village from which it took its name; it was in fact also the nearest station to the pleasant Dorset market town of Shaftesbury, just over two miles to the south. This picture shows D800 *Sir Brian Robertson* passing with the Sunday 4.15 Yeovil Town to Waterloo train on 6 March 1966. The lack of wagons in the goods yard and cattle dock siding was because general goods services had been withdrawn in April 1965, and indeed this was the last day that the station remained open for passengers. Just behind the third coach can be seen the 1961 signal box that had replaced the traditional LSWR box at the same position. Diesel-hydraulic D800 was built at Swindon in July 1958 and withdrawn after only ten years in October 1968.

By 16 February 1993 the scene has changed, as so often sadly for the worse. The main line here was singled in April 1967 and although the goods shed remains, the previously neat yard has now become an agricultural equipment scrapyard - an eyesore indeed. Vegetation encroaches down the cutting side on the left but the main station building still stands. The prominent tree behind the goods shed no longer obscures the now demolished chimney of the milk factory. However, the train at this time was still locomotive-hauled, with 33109 (in plain Departmental grey livery) hurrying past at the head of the 09.45 Exeter St Davids to Waterloo train. *M. Mensing/GR*

DEAN: Returning now to the east of Salisbury, this station, located in the village of West Dean, is situated right on the county boundary with Hampshire 9 miles from the city. It is on the line constructed from Eastleigh and Romsey, which when it was opened in January 1847 was the first railway to reach Salisbury. This 2 May 1964 photograph is looking westwards to Salisbury and shows LSWR cast iron lamp-posts, platform waiting shelters and signal box.

The station remains open for passenger trains and the main changes are the loss of signals, crossing gates, signal box and old station lamps. However, much else is as before on 24 June 1994, including the station house, vacant and awaiting a buyer. The Class '158' 'Express' unit is not stopping as it works the 10.30 Cardiff to Portsmouth service. *C. L. Caddy/GR*

DOWNTON was the first station on the Salisbury & Dorset Junction Railway, incorporated in 1861 to connect the Salisbury to Romsey line at Alderbury Junction with the 'Castleman Corkscrew' line at West Moors, west of Wimborne in Dorset. It was opened on 20 December 1866, worked from the start by the LSWR until absorbed by that concern in 1883. Other than a serious accident on 3 June 1884 south of Downton, in which five people were killed, this line had an uneventful existence, although it was sometimes used as a diversionary route to Bournemouth when necessary. In this 4 June 1960 scene, BR Standard Class '4' No 75067 is coming to a stop with the 8.22 pm Salisbury to Bournemouth Central train. Note that the down platform is disused, although surprisingly the footbridge remains, for it was as long ago as 1922 that Downton ceased to be a block section and crossing point. The line closed to all traffic on 4 May 1964.

It is difficult to visualise that a railway every existed here, as the station area has been redeveloped as a housing estate of pleasant bungalows. No evidence of the railway remains on 27 October 1993. *Hugh Ballantyne*

NEWTON TONY: Following the War Office decision to construct permanent military camps on Salisbury Plain, particularly on the south-east side, the LSWR sought a Light Railway Order to construct a branch line from Grateley to Amesbury, and subsequently opened it in 1901. This was the only original intermediate station until the branch was extended to Bulford in 1904, and in the same year a burrowing junction under the main line was built to enable through running to Salisbury. As one would expect with a Light Railway, the station was quite a modest affair, as this view looking toward Amesbury reveals. Although undated, the picture is thought to have been taken about 1914.

There was no trace of the station in April 1994, just a pile of manure and rubbish dumped on the site now owned by a local farmer. Beyond the road the trackbed gives vehicular access to adjacent fields. *Lens of Sutton collection/GR*

AMESBURY: For the military traffic here a very extensive goods yard and station with three platforms was built. This scene, looking south-east towards Newton Tony from the road overbridge on 24 September 1960, shows activity despite the closure to passenger traffic some eight years previously, the only evidence for that fact being the loop for the island platform having been reduced to a siding.

It is impossible to comprehend that this picture was taken from the same place on 30 March 1994. The whole area of the 'past' photograph near the railway bridge has been filled in to road level and become part of the London Road Industrial Estate. To the extreme left of the photograph is the road leading into the estate, which was the road going down to the yard on the extreme left of the 1960 picture. Today, infilling continues in the area beyond the old station footbridge. *R. M. Casserley/GR*

BULFORD: This view of the station, looking towards Bulford Camp, shows the single platform and the former signal box on the platform, which has been reduced to a ground frame. Beyond it Drummond 'M7' No 127 prepares to depart at 3.55 pm on its 14-mile journey to Salisbury, of which only 5³/₄ miles will be along the branch line. Soon after this picture was taken on 7 August 1950, the train service was reduced to a mere one per weekday, and obviously it could not survive. Passenger trains ceased on 30 June 1952, but goods continued until 4 March 1963.

Development has taken place and it is difficult to identify the location of the station, but the site is now part of a car park for commercial premises. 27 October 1993. *John Edgington/GR*

Salisbury area

SALISBURY (SR): This was the attractive railway setting visible from the end of the down main line platform looking west towards Salisbury 'B' signal box on the left, and in the far distance behind the train Salisbury SR loco shed. 'S15' Class No 30841 approaches the platforms heading towards London with a long goods train from Exmouth Junction on 27 August 1963. This locomotive was built at Eastleigh in July 1936 and withdrawn in January 1964; fortunately it was saved from Barry scrapyard and is now in working order on the North Yorkshire Moors Railway.

The 'present' photograph was taken on 22 March 1993, but has already been overtaken by events as far as the train is concerned because the smart rakes of coaches and locomotives in Network SouthEast livery have since been superseded by Class '159' 'Turbo' diesel units. Here, just before the changeover, No 47709 arrives at Salisbury hauling the 12.17 Exeter St Davids to Waterloo train. Despite the loss of the semaphore signals and box, and the sidings on the left, the simplified track layout is, by modern standards, reasonably extensive and maintains some railway atmosphere. *R. A. Lissenden/GR*

SALISBURY (SR) SHED: A view of three of the ten roads inside the shed looking west towards the buffers on 2 July 1967, in the very last week of Southern steam. To the left is No 34060 *25 Squadron* in steam, and on the right is the now nameless No 34098 *Templecombe*. Despite being relatively clean, this engine had been withdrawn a few weeks previously, but No 34060 survived another week after the photograph was taken to be included in the final batch of Southern steam withdrawals on 9 July 1967. All this Class of 'Light Pacifics' was built at Brighton, No 34060 in June 1947, rebuilt in November 1960, and No 34098 built in December 1949 and rebuilt in February 1961.

It proved very difficult to trace the exact position inside the shed on 21 February 1994, but this view of bushes in the large open area of what is now waste-ground is thought to be the correct spot. *Hugh Ballantyne/GR*

SALISBURY (SR), WEST END: Salisbury always was and remains the most important stop on the LSWR route between Waterloo and Exeter, although perhaps today in terms of ticket sales Basingstoke may now be in the lead. The LSWR reached Salisbury from Andover in May 1857, and this station at Fisherton, adjoining that of the GWR, was opened on 2 May 1859, which coincided with the opening day of the line from Salisbury to Yeovil, at that time owned by a company independent of the LSWR. All scheduled passenger trains stopped at the station except the 'Devon Belle' referred to on page 97. This 18 April 1964 picture will be familiar to those who recall the 1960s as typical of many years of Southern practice. Note the loco-spotter by the platform barrow and the long-armed Southern platform water column as No 34013 *Okehampton* makes ready to leave the down bay platform with the 3.05 pm local to Exeter. On the next track can be seen the bunker of 'M7' No 30025 on duty as the station pilot.

It is pleasing to report that BR have maintained Salisbury station to a very high order, and in recent years have carried out refurbishment of passenger facilities. Even the fine platform canopies remain, although the distinc-

tive Southern green end name-boards have gone and been replaced by corporate Network SouthEast platform signage. The two-storey building on the island platform, formerly a signal box, also remains, and the down plat-form bay is also still used. The only significant alteration on 6 December 1993 is the loss of the four sidings on the right, which have become part of the station car park. *Hugh Ballantyne/GR*

SALISBURY (SR), EAST END (1): The main Southern station in Wiltshire was always a good place to watch the action, and by standing on the long up bay platform, which extended well beyond the main platforms, one could enjoy sights such as this. While a 'Merchant Navy' sits in the up main platform with a Waterloo-bound train, 'Light Pacific' No 34057 *Biggin Hill* draws out with a Plymouth to Brighton train. Immediately on the right, part of the former Great Western station is visible, but by the date of this photograph, 27 August 1963, the connecting footbridge at the end of the Southern platforms had been removed. No 34057 was built at Brighton as 21C157 in March 1947 and withdrawn in May 1967.

Very little has changed in this scene over the intervening 30 years, with minimal track alterations - only the semaphore signals having been replaced. On 22 February 1993 a Class '47' can be seen in the distance at the far platform end and, centre background, part of the new servicing depot for the Class '159' 'Express' DMUs that replaced locomotive-hauled trains on the Waterloo to Exeter route in 1993. *R. A. Lissenden/GR*

SALISBURY (SR), EAST END (2): An interesting picture of the first main-line diesel-electric locomotive to be built for service in Great Britain seen at work on the Southern Region. No 10000 was LMS-designed by Mr H. G. Ivatt and the English Electric Co Ltd, and appeared right at the end of the LMS's independent existence in December 1947. It was a 1,600 hp locomotive and shortly afterwards, when its twin, No 10001, was built, the idea was to have the ability to produce a 3,200 hp unit with the pair working in tandem. In March 1953 No 10000 arrived on the Western Section of the Southern and was put to work on normal steam rosters. By May No 10001 had also arrived, and they worked, between teething troubles, diagrams on both the Bournemouth and Exeter routes. Here No 10000 comes round the tight curve into Salisbury station with the 1.00 pm Waterloo to Exeter express on 16 May 1953. Just in front of Salisbury East signal box, trailing away to the right, was the unique privately owned line of the Salisbury Railway & Market House Company. Opened in 1859, it was quite short, just half a mile in length, and despite its name carried mainly barley to the maltings adjacent to the track and coal to the local electricity generating works. The branch was always worked by its large neighbour, in later days the power being an

Ivatt 2-6-2T before it finally closed in July 1964. The track was lifted by December 1965 and the company went into voluntary liquidation in the same year.

At least the long bay platform remains, but much else has gone besides the Market House branch. The extensive sidings on the north side have disappeared, as has the signal box and associated semaphore signalling. No 37892, in two-tone grey livery and Trainload Petroleum Sector markings, brings 6V62, the Fawley to Tavistock Junction (Plymouth) oil tanks, towards the station on 18 November 1993. *E. W. Fry/GR*

SALISBURY TUNNEL: This is the approach to Salisbury from the east showing the cutting at the western end of Salisbury tunnel as the line curves towards the station. Class '7' 'Pacific' No 70020 *Mercury* is slowing for the station stop while working the Southern Counties Touring Society's 'South Western Rambler' special on 8 March 1964, which had started from Waterloo and visited Ludgershall in the course of its journey.

In the intervening years a new northern city bypass has been opened, which crosses the line by means of the now prominent bridge in this 22 March 1993 view. More housing development has also taken place out on the hillside to the left, and the former up relief line has been reduced to siding status as seen by the stop-block to the left of No 47705, which is approaching with the 11.15 Waterloo to Exeter St Davids train. *Hugh Ballantyne/GR*

SALISBURY (GWR): Following the construction of much of the Wilts, Somerset & Weymouth Railway, which then sold its assets to the Great Western on 14 March 1850, the GWR pressed ahead to complete the Westbury to Warminster line in 1851, with the remaining 19½ miles on to Salisbury opening for passenger traffic on 30 June 1856. The GWR terminus at Fisherton had an overall roof covering two platform roads and two centre sidings, giving the appearance of a small, neat and functional station. By the 1930s most of the trains from the Great Western worked beyond Salisbury and of necessity used the adjacent Southern station, so not surprisingly its own station was closed to passenger traffic on 12 September 1932. It then became relegated to goods traffic use, as seen here in this picture taken on 23 May 1957.

The station building still survives in commercial use and its roof can be seen centre and left. The prominent water tank continues to be a major landmark. 24 March 1994. *H. C. Casserley/GR*

118

SALISBURY (GWR) SHED: Following the opening of the line from Warminster to Salisbury in 1856, a loco shed was opened in 1858, but when the LSWR needed to remodel its adjacent congested station it paid the GWR to relocate from its station yard position to the north side of both companies' running lines near Ashfield Road. This shed opened in 1899, and comprised three roads; it was brick-built with a 'Northlight' slated and glazed roof, and was a typical Dean shed of the era. The coal stage with water tank above it is also clearly visible in this 21 May 1957 view, while beyond that a 65-foot diameter turntable was provided. It became a sub-shed to Westbury in 1932, and due to rationalisation, with Western engines using the Southern shed if required, it was closed on 26 November 1950 and subsequently demolished.

The site upon which the shed stood now forms part of the Ashfield Trading Estate, and industrial buildings cover the site, making direct visual comparison difficult. 24 March 1994. *H. C. Casserley/GR*

SALISBURY, MILFORD GOODS YARD: The first railway into Salisbury from Eastleigh ran to a terminus at Milford on the east side of city. Opened for goods in January 1847, passenger trains followed on 1 March of that year. This station remained in use until the Salisbury & Yeovil opened its station on the other side of the city, so when a new spur from Milford Junction and Fisherton Junction, later Tunnel Junction, connected the lines, Milford closed to passengers as long ago as 2 May 1859. However, the goods yard remained busy for over 100 years until it was eventually closed on 21 August 1967. Ivatt-designed Class '2' No 41320 is seen busily shunting the yard on a cold winter's day, 22 January 1965, in the yard's later years.

No trace of the goods yard or sidings remain visible on 24 June 1994. The point of reference is St Martin Church of England Junior School visible behind the wagons being shunted in the 'past' view, which are behind the trees and office block that today forms part of Milford Industrial Estate. At the entrance to the estate one can still obtain a drink at the Railway Inn. *Paul Strong/GR*

Midland & South Western Junction Railway

CRICKLADE, on the former Midland & South Western Junction Railway from Swindon Town to Cirencester, 8 miles 27 chains from the former, was opened on 18 December 1883. It was a modest country station with two platforms situated on a curve and a small goods yard on the north-east side with two main sidings. This picture, looking north towards Cirencester, shows the unusual sight of two LMS Class '2Ps' passing the station with an RCTS special, the 'East Midlander No 2' of 6 May 1956, which ran from Nottingham Midland to Swindon Junction via the Lickey incline and the M&SWJR hauled by No 40454, with the pilot engine No 40489 attached at Cheltenham Lansdown to Swindon. In the foreground is the small girder bridge No 116 by which means a footway went under the line.

The only way to identify the site on 13 December 1993 was by the footway under what has now become an access road in a housing estate. The 9 ft 9 in girder span bridge has been replaced by a concrete underpass, and it is difficult to believe that once a railway was located here. *Hugh Ballantyne/GR*

RUSHEY PLATT JUNCTION (1): A down main line goods train hauled by Collett '2884' Class No 3854 heads westwards over the diamond crossing taking the main line towards Wootton Bassett, $1^1/_2$ miles west of Swindon station, on 18 September 1955. The track leading to and from Swindon Town on the M&SWJR is that in the immediate foreground. To the left of the locomotive is the huge concentration yard at the western end of Swindon Works, and behind that a gantry crane near where 'C' Shop was situated and where withdrawn locomotives were sent for cutting up.

On 17 November 1993 there was little indication that this was the Great Western's connection with the M&SWJR. The deep-ballast main line between Swindon and Wootton Bassett sees a constant flow of HSTs, although the lineside has the now typical unkempt appearance with scrub and saplings in profusion on each side. The Railway Works concentration yard has completely disappeared and there is evidence of redevelopment in the left background. *R. C. Riley/GR*

RUSHEY PLATT JUNCTION (2): Further up the GWR/M&SWJR connecting line, looking north, part of the Swindon Works 'C' Shop complex and the concentration yard can again be seen in the background. On the left is Rushey Platt Station signal box with single line token apparatus visible on each side, serving both the high- and low-level tracks. The lines to the left formed part of the cross-country route from Andover to Andoversford; this section when built was known as the Swindon & Cheltenham Extension Railway and was opened, as far as Cirencester, for goods traffic on 1 November 1883 and for passengers on 23 June 1884. In that year the company amalgamated with the Swindon, Marlborough & Andover Railway to form the Midland & South Western Junction Railway. This junction had been built in 1881 by the SM&AR, but owing to a dispute with the GWR as to the working of trains between Swindon Junction and the SM&AR station at Swindon Town, it did not come into use until February 1882. Rushey Platt station had four platforms, the two lower ones on the spur to the GWR being staggered. The station closed as long ago as 1 October 1905, but some of the buildings remained in situ until the 1960s and were served by goods trains until 1964. The passenger train services over the M&SWJR had been substantially reduced by the Western Region in the 1950s and the remaining few trains were withdrawn from 9 September 1961. Goods traffic, mainly coal to Moreton Power Station, continued until 1973, and the track was finally lifted by 1978. This photograph shows Churchward 'Mogul' No 5396 coming round the spur off the GWR main line with a local train heading towards Swindon Town on 18 September 1955.

By 17 November 1993 nature had taken over, although the trackbeds of both lines are clearly visible, the M&SWJR line being used as a local footpath. Swindon Locomotive Works has now gone and modern development is visible in the distance to the right of the saplings now growing in profusion between the formation of the high- and low-level lines. *R. C. Riley/GR*

SWINDON TOWN was the focal point for the two north-south railways, the S&CER and SM&AR, which amalgamated on 23 June 1884 to become the Midland & South Western Junction Railway and promptly became bankrupt! When Sam Fay came from the LSWR in 1892 he successfully stimulated the growth of traffic and the railway settled down to provide a useful through route between the South of England and the Midlands, with military traffic to Tidworth also being important. Under the Railways Act of 1921 the railway was absorbed into the GWR, despite its strong associations with that company's rivals, the Midland and LSWR. In this picture North British-built 0-6-0PT No 7741 enters the station with the short 11.13 working from Swindon Junction on 6 December 1952. Note that four years after nationalisation the Pannier tank clearly displays the time-honoured initials 'GWR'. Built in 1930, this engine was withdrawn in December 1961 and sold to London Transport. It became LT No L96 for five years, working until December 1966 before finally being broken up at Neasden in September 1967.

Forty-one years later, on 16 December 1993, the station and railway have become an industrial estate, but one interesting relic of the M&SWJR's past history remains prominent. In both pictures on the left-hand side stands 'The Croft', a prominent building looking like a large house. This was, however, the offices of the M&SWJR and its appearance does not appear to have altered during the intervening years. *Hugh Ballantyne/GR*

CHISELDON station was located just over 3 miles south of Swindon Town and was well sited for the village on a curve in a cutting. It was a crossing station and a comparison with an early photograph shows that save for the rebuilding of the signal box the main station building and the waiting shelter on the down platform were little altered during the existence of the railway. 'Mogul' No 6334 is standing on the down line engaged in shunting wagons while working a southbound goods train on 15 March 1958. Opened on 27 July 1881, the station closed to all traffic on 11 September 1961.

Except for part of the bridge abutment wall on the left, no trace of the railway remains and the site is an open grassed amenity area. 28 February 1994. *H. C. Casserley/GR*

CHISELDON CAMP HALT: South of Chiseldon the M&SWJR traversed the Marlborough Downs at about the 500 feet contour, crossing somewhat bleak open downland. Typically in such a location the military decided to construct a camp nearby, called Draycott Camp, which in 1914 was served by a $1^1/_2$-mile-long siding but later closed. Subsequently, on 1 December 1930, a simple halt was constructed at a point on the line near to Draycott, and as can be seen it was a very simple affair with a short wooden platform and small shelter of corrugated iron sheeting. This picture is looking south towards Marlborough on 15 March 1958, the gradient here being a rising 1 in 300.

Another depressing scene on 28 February 1994, with builder's rubble dumped on part of the site with wild scrub gaining a firm hold despite the bleak open nature of the landscape hereabouts. The trackbed now forms part of a footpath from Chiseldon to Ogbourne. *H. C. Casserley/GR*

OGBOURNE: The line ran parallel to the old Roman Road, now the A345, for 3¹/₂ miles on a similarly straight course south from Chiseldon, and this was the next crossing station. There are several villages in the locality with Ogbourne in their names, but the station was situated in Ogbourne St George and was always just called Ogbourne. Its architectural features were similar to the other stations on this section of the M&SWJR, but it only had two short sidings on the east side, the shorter of which is prominent in this 14 May 1955 view, looking north towards Swindon.

Nothing remains of the station on 28 February 1994. Trees grow where once the elegant signal box stood on the up platform, and the footpath along the trackbed veers off the A365 at a point near the car, which is seen approximately where the station building was positioned. *R. C. Riley/GR*

MARLBOROUGH LOW LEVEL (1): Marlborough, an attractive little town west of Savernake Forest, is well known for its public school. It once boasted two railway stations close by one another; the High Level was the terminus of a branch from Savernake Low Level, which first arrived on the edge of the town in April 1864. Later, the projected Swindon to Andover line was, for economy, built in two parts, from Swindon to Marlborough and Savernake to Andover, and negotiated with the Marlborough Railway for running powers over the intervening gap. Understandably, two companies working trains over this short section proved unsatisfactory, and the M&SWJR, then managed by Sam Fay, decided to build its own line, so a new double track line to Savernake High Level, 5 miles long, was opened on 26 June 1898 and the M&SWJR became a useful link railway in the days before motor competition. Traffic rose to enormous tonnages during both World Wars, but by the 1950s it declined dramatically. The station is seen here from the Swindon end looking south as Churchward 'Mogul' No 6349 draws away with the lightly loaded 2.35 Andover Junction to Swindon Town local train, just a two coach 'B set', on 8 June 1954.

On 13 December 1993 there is only this depressing view in the Kennet District Council's yard, in which no trace of the M&SWJR station remains. *Hugh Ballantyne/GR*

MARLBOROUGH LOW LEVEL (2): In this picture, looking north, Maunsell Class 'U' No 31619 has a clear road to proceed with an Andover Junction to Cheltenham St James train, while in the background a Pannier tank waits with its two-coach 'B set' for the shuttle service to Savernake on 29 August 1959. The station closed to passengers on 10 September 1961 and to goods traffic with effect from 7 September 1964.

On 15 December 1993 two Ford lorries stand on the spot where the elegant 'Mogul' had been - a sad sight

indeed, showing the former railway and station as a Kennet District Council yard. Only the row of houses in left background and the slope of Posterne Hill on the extreme north-western edge of Savernake Forest establish that it is the same location. *M. Crump/GR*

MARLBOROUGH LOW LEVEL (3): Looking north into the station on 7 August 1950, bunting decorates the station canopy (reason not known) and the neat layout of a country station, which even boasted a refreshment room, can be seen. Churchward-designed 'Mogul' No 5367 heads into the evening sun departing with the 6.30 pm Swindon Town to Andover Junction train.

Today this part of the station forms the approach road to Kennet District Council's yard, and again no evidence of the railway remains. 13 December 1993. *John Edgington/GR*

MARLBOROUGH HIGH LEVEL station was the terminus of a 5-mile branch from Savernake Low Level, promoted as the Marlborough Railway and later absorbed into the Great Western. It opened for traffic on 14 April 1864 as a broad gauge line and was converted to standard gauge ten years later, in June 1874, at the same time as the Berks & Hants line of the GWR was converted. When the M&SWJR opened its own line between Marlborough Low Level and Savernake High Level in 1898, it thus duplicated the service. However, it was not until 6 March 1933 that the station was closed to passengers. The connection with the Low Level station remained and goods trains still had access until the station was closed to all traffic on 19 May 1964. In this 1 September 1952 picture the traffic is obviously very light, but it shows the station building to good advantage, the ornate water tank and, behind the loading gauge, the single-road loco shed.

Nothing remains of this attractive railway backwater on 17 February 1994, landscaping and development having completely obliterated the station. Clear evidence that this was the correct location, however, are the two semi-detached houses on the left of each picture. *H. C. Casserley/GR*

SAVERNAKE HIGH LEVEL: Due to the unsatisfactory arrangements imposed by the GWR upon the M&SWJR and its predecessor, the Swindon, Marlborough & Andover Railway, the Marlborough & Crofton Railway was promoted to avoid using the GWR's Marlborough Railway branch. The new railway was a 6¾-mile double-track line and included this one intermediate station, 200 yards north of the Great Western station and opened for traffic on 26 June 1898. However, by the 1920s the Great Western, having two routes open between Marlborough and Savernake, was looking for economies, and alterations were duly made by 1933. Most trains subsequently used the Low Level station, although two M&SWJR services continued to run through this station using the up platform only until 1958. The down line was reduced to a loop and the signal box downgraded to a ground frame to become Savernake Middle Ground Frame as seen here on 6 April 1957, with No 6349 entering the station hauling the 4.38 pm Southampton Terminus to Cheltenham Lansdown train.

The High Level station has become a private residence and in what is now the garden several relics of the railway remain, not least the shell of the lovely little M&SWJR signal box as seen here. It is emphasised that the signal box is on private land and that this photograph was taken with the owner's kind permission expressly granted in advance of the visit on 23 June 1994. Readers are advised that visitors are not welcome and should not disturb the owner or attempt to trespass on his property. *Neil Spinks/GR*

GRAFTON JUNCTION was the southern end of the new linking line that enabled M&SWJR trains to pass north-wards unimpeded by the Great Western, which caused delays and levied excessive rate charges on the former Marlborough Railway. Seen here on 29 August 1959, the line to the left curves down to the GWR at Wolfhall Junction (see page 78), while the line ahead leads to Savernake High Level station after crossing the Kennet & Avon Canal and the GWR's Berks & Hants main line.

The line of the embankment and railway route remain discernable on 6 April 1994, but grass and scrub have taken over where the once well-kept permanent way (what a misnomer!) was laid. *M. Crump/GR*

GRAFTON SOUTH JUNCTION, a little further on, was where the double-track Grafton curve of 44 chains length led up from the Berks & Hants line to the right. This curve was opened on 6 September 1905 and under an agreement gave the GWR running powers to Ludgershall. The curve never had a regular passenger service and was closed on 5 May 1957. This excellent view of the junction on 8 July 1956 shows a train coming south from Savernake towards Ludgershall on the 'main' line hauled by No 6372; this was the RCTS 'Wessex Wyvern' special, which had originated from Waterloo and travelled to Portland, returning via Westbury and Devizes. It had just come on to the M&SWJR over the connection from Wolfhall Junction shown opposite. Resplendent in lined green livery, No 6372 hauled this train between Weymouth Town and Andover Junction.

What a contrast! The site of this splendid railway junction layout is now a farm manure dump and, indeed, our intrepid photographer had to stand on top of a load of manure to take this picture on 8 November 1993 because the road overbridge from which No 6372 was photographed has now been filled in. The tree in the centre middle distance equates to the position of the South Junction signal box. *Les Elsey/GR*

GRAFTON & BURBAGE was the first station on the southern section of the Swindon, Marlborough & Andover Railway, which opened on 1 May 1882, albeit only for local traffic towards Andover; it was not until 5 February 1883, following agreement with the GWR regarding traffic via Savernake, that through running of trains to and from Swindon commenced. In 1902 doubling of the line between Collingbourne and this station meant that there was continuous double track for $17^3/_4$ miles between Weyhill and Marlborough. This picture, looking north on 15 March 1958, shows the station name simply as 'Grafton', but this was not its official title. The GWR-style $12^1/_2$ milepost on the up platform is the measurement from Red Post Junction at the point where the M&SWJR met the Southern main line west of Andover. Maunsell Class 'U' No 31639 is coming into the down platform with probably one of the three daily through trains between Cheltenham and Southampton.

The station building and platform canopy have now been incorporated into an attractive residence and the trackbed between the platforms infilled to form part of the gardens in front of the station. The platform area at the south end from where the 'past' picture was taken has become a paddock. This photograph was taken on 8 November 1993 with the kind permission of the owner of the house. *R. C. Riley/GR*

COLLINGBOURNE KINGSTON HALT: From Grafton the M&SWJR continued southwards on generally falling gradients, and after 2³/₄ miles, on coming into the valley of the little River Bourne, reached this halt. It was opened on 1 April 1932 and was situated in this small village close to the A338 road to Andover in an attempt to combat road competition. It was a simple structure, short wooden platforms and the usual corrugated sheeting shelters. On 17 April 1961, in the last few months of operation, when the through train service was reduced to just one daily train, Eastleigh-allocated Standard Class '4' 'Mogul' No 76028 pulls away with the 1.52 pm Cheltenham to Southampton train. On 11 September 1961 the halt was closed with the rest of the M&SWJR stations.

By 20 April 1994 undergrowth has taken over the site of the halt, but railway fencing on the east boundary remains. The minor road overbridge, prominent in the past picture, but now partly hidden by the bushes, has required a strengthening pillar to support its weakening structure, which today serves no useful purpose. *Colin G. Maggs/GR*

COLLINGBOURNE was another station constructed when the railway was opened on 1 May 1882, being 4¼ miles south of Grafton and situated in the village of Collingbourne Ducis. The neatness of the track and lineside is again readily apparent in this study of Churchward 'Mogul' No 6320 setting out from the station with an afternoon train from Swindon to Andover on 8 July 1956. This locomotive was built at Swindon in February 1921 and withdrawn in November 1963.

This once attractive part of the railway is now reduced to levelled ground used by a local farmer as a dump for materials and a pile of manure in the centre of the picture. Not visible, but apparent on site, are the platforms albeit filled in. The old station approach road continues to give access to the land, and on the extreme left the station house remains as a residence on 30 March 1994. *R. C. Riley/GR*

LUDGERSHALL (1): Although only a village, this was the largest station on the M&SWJR, covering a site of some 16 acres. Situated just inside the county boundary on the edge of Salisbury Plain, it served a major region of military camps and its size represented the importance the railway played in assisting the military in the transportation of vast quantities of men and materials over the years. The station had five platforms, two through lines as seen in this picture, north- and south-end bays and a double-ended bay on the down (north) side. A particular feature was the enormous width of the platforms, designed to accommodate troops and equipment and give them space in getting on and off trains. The platform buildings were relatively small, but were connected by a substantial latticework-sided footbridge with awning, under part of which 'U' Class 'Mogul' No 31629 is arriving with a Southampton to Cheltenham train on 9 July 1954. The station closed to passenger traffic with the rest of the

M&SWJR stations on 11 September 1961, but sees occasional military traffic on the remnant of that railway which remains from Andover.

Except for the one running line and loop giving access to the military sidings on part of the truncated Tidworth branch, nothing of the station remains on 2 February 1994, save the up platform brick edging and, incongruously, the concrete lamp standard shown on the right of the 'past' picture! Housing development has completely altered the landscape upon which the large station once stood.
R. C. Riley/GR

LUDGERSHALL (2): The view looking northwards across the wide up platform shows the spacious layout of this large station. A small crowd of onlookers has gathered to watch a rare visiting locomotive class to the line, three years after passenger traffic had ceased, in the form of Standard Class '7' No 70020 *Mercury*. The date is 8 March 1964, and the 'Britannia' was working a Southern Counties Touring Society special from Waterloo, and had just run round its train in order to go back to Andover Junction and regain the main line to Salisbury.

Only the up platform edging remains partly visible in the centre left background, together with the two tracks that formerly would have been the main up and down running lines. To the left landscaping has been carried out, and to the right semi-detached houses occupy the greater part of the old station site on 24 June 1994. In the right background some solid brick-built buildings and chimney stacks, visible behind the telegraph pole in the 'past' scene, remain. *Hugh Ballantyne/GR*

TIDWORTH (1): Following the development of a large military camp at Tidworth, the M&SWJR approached the War Office about building a railway from Ludgershall to serve the camp. This was agreed in 1900 and a railway just over 2 miles long, built on War Office land, was opened for military manoeuvres traffic on 8 July 1901. Shortly afterwards the War Department allowed the branch to become a public railway, and it was worked on this basis by the M&SWJR, opening for goods on 1 July 1902 and to passengers on 1 October 1902. It was leased by the M&SWJR and its successors until the public passenger service was withdrawn on 19 September 1955, after which traffic was handled by the War Department itself until closure on 31 July 1963. Part of the line remains open towards the Ludgershall end and trains are run as required. As can be seen in this photograph, the station had two long platforms with a run-round release road and water columns at the platform ends. Extensive sidings were provided for the substantial traffic, both military and civilian, the latter especially generated at the time of the Tidworth Tattoo, which brought excursion trains from far and wide. Shortly before withdrawal of the passenger service, No 5396 is making ready to run tender-first with two coaches as the 4.45 pm to Ludgershall, the last train of the day, on 7 September 1955.

This is another location where redevelopment has completely changed the area. After some difficulty a view from the end of the NAAFI building, on the extreme left, found the correct angle of the chimney above the houses, which is just behind the bottom left-hand end gable of the station building in the 'past' scene, thereby giving the correct perspective for the 30 March 1994 photograph. *Hugh Ballantyne/GR*

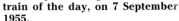

TIDWORTH (2): This time the 'Mogul' is facing towards Ludgershall, as No 6320 prepares to leave Tidworth station with the 4.45 to Ludgershall on 1 September 1952. By the 1950s the passenger train service was just a meagre three trains each way on weekdays, worked out and back from Ludgershall.

This was another picture that presented difficulty in pin-pointing some 'past' features to give accuracy to the picture alignment on 30 March 1994. New roads and terraced houses, with the NAAFI building at 90 degrees in the background, caused a problem, but in the gap between the right-hand end of the NAAFI and the house on the extreme right are some gateposts that are also visible in the background to the right of the station building in the 'past' scene. *H. C. Casserley/GR*

INDEX OF LOCATIONS